LONDON

THE DOCTRINE
OF OUR REDEMPTION

by

NATHANIEL MICKLEM

PRINCIPAL OF MANSFIELD COLLEGE, OXFORD

with an Introduction by

THE ARCHBISHOP OF CANTERBURY

LONDON
EYRE & SPOTTISWOODE, LTD.
14, 15, & 16 BEDFORD STREET, W.C.2

CONTENTS

INTRODUCTION

BY

THE MOST REVEREND
THE ARCHBISHOP OF CANTERBURY

IT is the purpose of this series to assist thoughtful devotion and devotional thought. The last volume had insisted on the helplessness of man apart from the redeeming love of God. It was therefore right to follow it by a volume setting forth the doctrine of our redemption.

I was glad to secure Dr. Micklem as the author, partly in order to illustrate the fact that, as he puts it, "There is not, and there never has been, any controversy between the Church of England and Orthodox Dissent in respect of the articles of the Christian Faith," but chiefly because no one is better qualified than he is for the task.

There is no one official or authoritative theory of Redemption. All Christian theology is the attempt to reach a fuller understanding of it or to throw some new light upon it by a fresh approach. But all the theologies together are needed for a full apprehension of it, and at the end they leave us with more that is unexplored than what is known.

Yet the central significance is always the same, and can be, as it often is, experienced by the simple soul to whom every theology would bring only bewilderment. He "loved me and gave Himself for me"—that is the perfectly simple statement of what contains "unsearchable riches."

Dr. Micklem shows how Christians in different parts of the world and different epochs of history have approached this central theme in accordance with their own general experience or the prevalent habits of contemporary (to each age "modern") thought. They have always seen something and missed much. As we try, under Dr. Micklem's guidance, to see through their eyes we shall learn something that we should miss if we used only our own. And as he closes he points to a great extension of the doctrine, for which the New Testament and the Christian tradition supply the grounds, but which our own experience is leading us to emphasize with quite new urgency.

WILLIAM CANTUAR:

CANTERBURY

September 9, 1942

PREFACE

A PREFACE should, I think, be addressed to the man who picks up a volume in a bookshop and wishes to know at a glance whether it is likely to be of interest to him. A writer, therefore, should set forth in his preface the aim he sets before himself and perhaps be allowed to explain what he is not attempting.

The title of this little book is clear, but it may suggest an enterprise altogether beyond my powers. This is not another text-book dealing historically with the various doctrines of the Atonement; still less does it offer some novel doctrine of my own. Nor, on the other hand, does it belong to the class of edifying literature addressed rather to the heart and the feelings than to the head. It is written to stimulate thought and thereby, if it please God, quicken devotion also. I have had in mind two types of reader in particular, first, the many groups of lay people, men and women, up and down the country who "wish they knew a little more theology" and who desire better to understand the faith which they profess. Second, the ordained minister too busy with the multifarious duties of his office to find time for more weighty volumes and thus in some danger of getting into a theological rut.

I have written of St. John of Damascus and St. Augustine and St. Anselm and St. Thomas Aquinas and Luther and other great names in the story of Christian thought. But I have not intended or attempted a learned and systematic exposition of their thought. I have merely picked out points here and there either because they are apt to be forgotten, or because they seem to have a special relevance to our present spiritual and intellectual need. This, then, is not a systematic treatise. It will, however, fulfil its humbler purpose if it serve to enlarge the reader's thought, to quicken his imagination, and to lead him to a greater wonder. The Greeks used to speak of "worshipping the divine with other people's incense." That would be a good motto for my unpretentious book.

If I have written nothing here about the "redemption" of society, this is not because I deem the subject unimportant. Indeed, if the Gospel is to be commended to the modern world, it must certainly be related to our economic and social life. In this book, however, I am only concerned with the work of God in the soul of man.

I have written at the bidding of the Archbishop of Canterbury. Many-besides myself will be astonished at his choice of a writer; but it serves as a happy reminder that, in spite of all differences of churchmanship, there is not, and there never has been, controversy between the Church of England and Orthodox Dissent in respect of the articles of the Christian faith.

N. M.

THE PRINCIPAL'S LODGINGS,
MANSFIELD COLLEGE, OXFORD

CHAPTER I

What is Redemption?

In this introductory chapter we first consider the way in which the doctrine of our redemption is related to the Bible, to the Church and to personal religious experience. Then the meaning of the term "Redemption," as it concerns this life, is illustrated by various quotations. Next it is pointed out that redemption must be consummated beyond this world, and the question is raised whether our preoccupation with our own salvation would be selfish. Finally an attempt is made to indicate the mystery of our redemption.

For further reading the following books may be suggested: (1) *What is Salvation?* by E. S. Waterhouse (Hodder & Stoughton); (2) *The Atonement*, three lectures by the Bishop of Gloucester (Hodder & Stoughton); (3) the chapters by Doctors Whale and Wheeler Robinson on Redemption in *The Christian Faith*, edited by the Dean of St. Paul's (Eyre & Spottiswoode); (4) *The Nature of Sanctity*, by Ida von Coudenhove (Sheed & Ward); (5) *They Found God*, a series of biographical studies by M. L. Christlieb (Allenson); (6) *Sister Eva of Friedenshort* (Hodder & Stoughton).

Questions that would naturally arise for discussion are such as these: (1) What is the relation between the authority of the Bible and of the Church? (2) How far is religious experience necessary to the understanding of the Christian faith? (3) Do you think that the experience illustrated in Section II ought to be common to all Christians? (4) What is your idea of heaven? (5) Could you be happy in heaven without your family? (6) Can we speak of the death of our Lord as "a world catastrophe"?

THIS book is addressed to Christians who want to understand their faith. In the sphere of apologetics the Church presents its case to the world; in dogmatic theology the Church cross-questions itself about its own life. That we are redeemed "by the blood of Christ," to use St. Paul's historic phrase, is part of the universal confession of the whole Church catholic. We use the words sincerely, but only very partially do we understand them. We may not hope to find a theory to embrace the infinite or explain in adequate and tidy terms exactly what has been done for us by Christ. Our redemption by the Incarnation of the Son of God is unfathomable mystery. But this does not mean that it is unintelligible or irrational, only that "the love of God is broader than the measures of man's mind." That Christ died for our sins we all confess, but the Church is committed to no one theory or doctrine or explanation of redemption. In this book we are concerned, not with a systematic, or even an historical, exposition of the Atonement, but with "moments" or aspects or intuitions which must all be taken up when God is pleased to give us a new St. Thomas Aquinas to sum up the wisdom so far attained.

I

We speak of our redemption, but what do we mean by redemption, and how do we know that we are redeemed? In answering these questions some point us to the Bible, some to the Church, and some to personal experience. Each of these answers is true so far as it goes, but none is wholly satisfactory without the others. We will consider them in turn.

(1) The Bible is the Word of God to us because it declares the Gospel. The Gospel is Good News. The Good News is the message of our redemption by the Incarnate Son of God who "died for our sins and rose again for our justification." We believe the Good News, and we derive from the Bible both the definition and the assurance of redemption. This is true and fundamental, but it is not all.

(2) We cannot safely separate the Gospel from the Church, for the Church, in spite of all its sins, is a part or a continuation of the Gospel. The choice and the schooling and disciplining of Israel is followed "in the fulness of times" by the coming of the Messiah. There is no break. The death and Resurrection of our Lord are followed by Pentecost and therewith the mission of the Church; again, there is no break. The Good News is fully and finally declared in Scripture, yet there is no moment at which we can say, "Here the Good News ends." We may say, if we will, that the Gospel culminates in the coming of the Holy Ghost. But the Holy Ghost is not come and gone; once again, there is no break. On the night of his betrayal our Lord

broke the bread and took the cup, and said, "This is my Body. . . . This cup is the new covenant in my Blood." From that day to this not a week has passed, perhaps not a day has passed, but the Church has taken the cup and known her Lord in the breaking of the bread. This mysterious thing that happened on Calvary and on Easter morning is not isolated and cut off from us by ever-lengthening tracts of hurrying time. Not the mere memory of it but the thing itself is brought down into our present and to our hearts and to our very lips. We believe the Gospel because we are in the life that proceeds from the Gospel; that which otherwise would be incredible we believe because we are in the Church. But this leads naturally and inevitably to our third answer.

(3) A man might very well say of the Good News, "the Bible says so, the Church says so, but I do not believe a word of it; why should I?" No man can believe the mystery of the Gospel unless there be in his heart what the Reformers called "the inward testimony of the Holy Ghost." Some element of "experience" is necessary. In these days of psychologizing we are wary of this word "experience." Our feelings, indeed, are no compass to steer by. We are not good because we feel good, and we are not saved or redeemed because of our emotional experiences. Yet the answer of the heart there must be, or we cannot believe and come home to God.

We have attained, then, to a very tentative and preliminary answer to our questions. By redemption we mean the Good News which is declared in Scripture, which, to some extent at least, is realized in the life of the Church, and which through the Bible and the Church has in some degree come home to us. We rest our assurance of redemption, not on our own private experiences nor on the experiences of other people nor yet upon a Book which we credulously accept, but upon all these together in mutual tension and support. Our own dim, individual experience is of little significance for the doctrine of our Redemption, yet apart from it the doctrine has for us no meaning.

II

"By thy Cross and precious Blood thou hast redeemed us"—
that is the confession of the Church. But what precisely is
meant by "redeemed" in this connection? The mode of our
redemption may be a mystery too deep for our understanding,
but we must know, in part at least, the nature or content of
that which we call redemption. It has two *foci*; it is related both
to this world and to that which is to come. When we ask what
redemption means in this world, we should be unwise to limit
our inquiries to our own very partial and disappointing spiritual
attainments; we shall do better to look at one of those of whom
men spontaneously say, "He is a *real* Christian." If we were
asked to define a Christian, we might say that he is a baptized
person who has not repudiated his baptism, but a more satisfactory definition will be in terms of what a Christian ought to
be if he fully realizes his nature as a Christian. So now we will
ask what redemption may mean even now in this world, but
we shall not imply that those whose attainment or experience
falls short of what is possible are therefore not in the company
of the redeemed.

Perhaps redemption may be more satisfactorily indicated
by illustration than by exposition—at least by way of introduction.

(1) Paul wrote to the Church in Corinth: "Be not deceived;
neither fornicators nor idolaters nor adulterers nor effeminate
nor abusers of themselves with mankind nor thieves nor covetous
nor drunkards nor revilers nor extortioners shall inherit the
Kingdom of God. And such were some of you; but ye are
washed, but ye are sanctified, but ye are justified in the name
of the Lord Jesus, and by the Spirit of our God." Redemption
is deliverance from sin and uncleanness to purity and holiness.
This experience has been lyrically expressed in some of the
great hymns:

> He breaks the power of cancelled sin;
> He sets the prisoner free;
> His blood can make the foulest clean;
> His blood availed for me. . . .

4

> Jesus, the Name that charms our fears,
> That bids our sorrows cease,
> 'Tis music in the sinners ears;
> 'Tis life and health and peace.

This is culled from a hymn by Charles Wesley; it may be taken as a typical expression of what is called "the evangelical experience," which would be an excellent name for it except that, unfortunately, the word "evangelical" like the word "catholic" has sometimes been stolen for party purposes, and this ecstatic hymnody of Charles Wesley has its closest counterpart in some of those hymns of the medieval Church which are connected with St. Bernard's name. This deliverance from sin, then, is part of what redemption means, or may mean, even in this world.

(2) One night, we are told, William Canton was reading in bed some latest work on Christian theology; he was oppressed, it seems, with the problems, difficulties and obscurities of the subject. He fell asleep, and in the morning he was awakened by a ploughman singing beneath his window—a common ploughman with a hard day's work ahead of him and no likely respite in this world. This is what the ploughman was singing:

> My God, the spring of all my joys,
> The life of my delights,
> The glory of my brightest days,
> And comfort of my nights.
>
> In darkest shades, if He appear,
> My dawning is begun!
> He is my soul's sweet morning star,
> And He my rising sun.

The transfiguration of the common life, so that it is no more commonplace nor drudgery but a glad and free offering in love to God is one of the universal marks of redemption in every age and every denomination. Perhaps the best-known example is that of Brother Lawrence, but George Herbert is another:

> Who sweeps a room as for Thy laws
> Makes that and the action fine.

For the redeemed an uncommon light shines upon common things. Further, that which is hard for the flesh is made joy in the Spirit. "If thou carry the cross," said St. Thomas à Kempis, "the cross shall carry thee."

Of this a signal but very typical illustration is the girl Armelle who in 1696 was born the daughter of the peasant George Nicolas at Campenac in France. All her life she was a servant. "Armelle's mistress," writes Miss Christlieb, "began to pile one labour after another upon the sick girl, at the same time ordering her fellow-servant to spare her in nothing, but to leave the hardest jobs always to her. From morning till night Armelle now had never a moment's rest, in spite of her feverish condition. One day, utterly exhausted, she fainted. Her mistress insisted that it was all imagination, and that more work was the cure. She now made her fetch water from a distant spring outside the town. The carrying of the large vessel on her head caused the girl intolerable pain. . . . Nothing she did was right. Over every task she was scolded and found fault with." It seems clear from the record that she was treated with shocking cruelty. "It seemed to me," she said, "my sufferings were nothing to what I desired to suffer following the example of Christ. His image was ever before my eyes; as he was instructing me inwardly as a teacher and I was listening to his voice as a pupil, always seeking to learn from him, I scarcely took heed of how I was treated outwardly. I was shut in with myself; I held on to the divine Love, and did not lose sight of his Presence. I conversed with him, rejoiced to suffer a little for him, and asked him for a measure of that patience he showed in his own earthly life." Redemption then is, or may be, victory over the world, over its drudgery and over its suffering. It is reconciliation, not only with God, but also with the life which God has appointed for us.

(3) Our redemption covers both the work of Christ for us and the work of his Holy Spirit in us. Redemption is a process as well as a fact. It is sometimes traditionally put in this way: the death of Christ for our sins is applied to us in our baptism; after that, we must walk the purgative, the illuminative and the unitive way. Redemption, as we may know it now, implies a

union of the soul with God. "Upon a day," wrote John Bunyan, "the good providence of God called me to Bedford, to work on my calling; and in one of the streets of that town, I came where there were three or four poor women sitting at a door, in the sun, talking about the things of God; and being now willing to hear their discourse, I drew near to hear what they said, for I was now a brisk talker of myself in the matters of religion; but I may say, 'I heard but understood not,' for they were far above, out of my reach. Their talk was about a New Birth, the Work of God in their hearts, as also how they were convinced of their miserable state by nature; they talked how God had visited their souls with his love in the Lord Jesus, and with what Words and Promises they had been refreshed, comforted and supported against the temptations of the devil."

This testimony of the "three or four poor women" is, no doubt, couched in the phraseology of the seventeenth century in England, but in substance it might have come from St. Augustine or St. Bernard or St. Bonaventura, from Cincinnati or from Tokyo. This is the language of the redeemed which echoes and re-echoes down the Christian centuries. Some have spoken of infused grace, others of the workings of the Holy Spirit, others of regeneration, others of sanctification—

> Ten thousand thousand are their tongues,
> But all their joys are one.

I have not attempted a scientific or theological account of what redemption means in this life, and I have repudiated the suggestion that a man who has none of these seraphical experiences is therefore not among the redeemed. But it is right and necessary when we set out to consider the doctrine and mystery of our redemption that we should contemplate the grace of God not merely in our own meagre experience but also in the saints.

"The grace of God"—this word "grace," which will recur, needs explanation. In the New Testament it has two chief meanings. First, it is a name for God's gracious attitude and relationship to us; it expresses the outgoing of his love to us,

7

especially it is his forgiving and redeeming love. Thus we speak of "the grace of our Lord Jesus Christ." Second, "grace" is the new relationship to God and to one another, the new world, into which Christ brings us; this is "the grace in which we stand." In old days a child misbehaving at table was often made to stand in the corner and thus "put in disgrace." Grace is the opposite of dis-grace; it is the family circle restored; it is the sphere of reconciliation and mutual joy in the family of God. In the Middle Ages and in modern Roman Catholic books grace is used in a third sense; it is applied to the working of the Holy Spirit in our hearts. All these meanings are closely connected, but in this book "grace" will be taken in the New Testament senses and mean either the outgoing of God's forgiving love to us in Christ or the new world of the reconciled family of God into which we are brought by Christ.

III

There is a "finished" work of Christ; he died once for all; God has visited and has redeemed his people. Yet the work of redemption is not yet complete, nor can it be till the Consummation. Redemption, therefore, is connected essentially with the life to come. What it means in this connection obviously cannot be indicated by illustration, and the metaphors and picture language in which men have tried to express that beatitude which it hath not entered into the heart of man to conceive are not altogether helpful. The true end of man, as St. Thomas Aquinas would put it, is to behold the vision of God; the chief end of man, as the Reformers put it, is "to glorify God and enjoy him for ever."

Here the greatest difficulty is not the poverty of our language to picture heaven but our spiritual numbness or superficiality. We talk, sometimes even jestingly, of "going to heaven"; we know that we cannot picture heaven, and therefore we put all serious thought of it from our minds. Heaven is popularly supposed to be a place or a state that will be very, very nice, and we are content to leave it at that. Heaven a nice place? The problem is how it could be endurable for one moment to any one of us. We are to behold the face of God in glory; we are to appear before him with every veil removed; is this a tolerable thought?

> O how shall I, whose native sphere
> Is dark, whose mind is dim,
> Before the Ineffable appear,
> And on my naked spirit bear
> That uncreated beam?

We are to be at home with God, and how can such as we are be at home with God? "They shall see him whom they have pierced." If our Lord were to look upon us with those eyes with which he looked upon St. Peter in the hall, should we be in heaven or in hell? We do not begin to see the mystery of our redemption till we apprehend it as something incredible, impossible, beyond all reason and thought, and yet made possible and reasonable and actual and near in Jesus Christ our Lord. John Keble wrote of the sense of awe with which he approached the sacrament:

> It is my Maker—dare I stay?
> My Saviour—dare I turn away?

So Newman speaks of "these two pains, so counter and so keen," the longing and the dread. "O that I knew where I might find him, that I might come even to his seat"—"no man can see God and live"; "depart from me, O Lord, for I am a sinful man"—"forsake me not, O Lord, be not far from me." There will be no doctrine, because there will be no apprehension, of redemption unless redemption be seen as something "almost too wonderful to be."

The Christian's interest in the ultimate salvation of his soul is sometimes said to be a selfish preoccupation. That is a shallow judgment, but perhaps it contains a grain of truth. Salvation is, indeed, a personal matter; it is through faith and charity; religion is the intercourse of "the alone with the Alone." Therefore, whether in the language of the cloister or of the evangelistic campaign, redemption has been conceived as an individual matter. Such it must be, but it may well be doubted whether, when set forth in purely individualistic terms, it is adequate to the full thought of the New Testament. In what sense is Christ the Saviour of the world, of the whole Universe, as St. Paul suggests? In this present age, when our sense of corporate life and social responsibility is being quickened, we shall do well especially to reconsider the hints of Scripture and Church doctrine as to the universal scope of the work of Christ.

IV

St. Anselm's famous writing on the Atonement is called "Why the God-man?" or "Why did God become man?" He did not ask *whether* God became man. In these pages similarly we are assuming and presupposing the Christian faith and seeking only to understand it better. To argue about the faith is easy and, under certain circumstances, delightful; that is an exercise of wits, and some never get beyond it; for it is fatally easy to use the articles and affirmations of the Christian faith as counters in an intellectual game. Thus it often happens that men will assert the most overwhelming and soul-shattering truths as if they were the merest commonplaces. That "Christ died for our sins" we all admit, we take it for granted, we have known it since we were children. But suppose we put the emphasis on the first word and try to imagine what it means that *Christ* died. This is how Professor Karl Adam puts it:

> The glad tidings of the Resurrection are also the glad tidings of the Atonement. The Easter light throws its clarifying rays on Golgotha and on the Cross. It is only by this light that we can unveil and interpret that mystery which to the Jews was a stumbling-block and to the Gentiles a foolishness. We are not merely fronted by the heroic act of a holy person obedient unto death to the heavenly Father, but by the death of a man who is God, by the death of our Lord, by the death of one who is to judge the world. It is an event so dreadful, so past all conception, that the sun pales in the heavens, the earth quakes, and the veil of the temple is rent from top to bottom. Something cosmic is happening here, a world catastrophe. The God-Man is dying. We know very well that God, in himself, cannot die. But it is not God as such, who is dying: it is a man substantially united to the Word of God, a man who *is* God.

10

It is often observed that a new note of wonder is being heard from the men of modern science who probe the unimaginable spaces of the universe or consider the infinitesimal marvels and complexities of the immeasurably small and beautiful. When they think of God at all, they seem in awe before his power. The time is perhaps at hand when the interest of men will be less exclusively upon the external world; then, it may be, in the Cross of the Son of God they will see the love of God as immeasurable, as inconceivable as his power in nature. When we contemplate the death of the Son of God, we are as men looking dizzily into the abyss, the abyss of charity and grace, the mystery of our redemption.

CHAPTER II

The Old Testament Foundation

Christian doctrine rests upon the Holy Scriptures of the Old and New Testaments. In this chapter we consider some aspects of the teaching of the Old Testament about redemption. First, our redemption is a matter of divine covenant and promise. Second, it was the purpose of God through the Hebrews to make known his salvation to all the earth. Third, the Old Testament tells of the beginnings of the Church, which is the sphere of redemption. Fourth, it is noted that many of the titles of our Lord taken from the Old Testament are open to a corporate interpretation and thus suggest that he is the Head of the new humanity. Fifth, we consider in what sense the Old Testament predicts Christ. Sixth, we consider in particular the Songs of the Servant in Isaiah.

The most important reading to be suggested is the Old Testament itself. The chapter headings given in many editions of the Authorized Version indicate the Christian interpretation of the Old Testament. They deserve careful consideration. Fr. G. Hebert's *The Throne of David* is to be commended (S.P.C.K.), also a pamphlet by H. Cunliffe-Jones called *The Old Testament as a Standard and Rule of Christian Faith* (Methodist Sacramental Fellowship), also the chapters on the Bible and the Church by Canon Mozley and myself in *The Christian Faith*, edited by the Dean of St. Paul's (Eyre & Spottiswoode), and by John Morgan Jones, *The Revelation of God in the Old Testament*.

Questions that would naturally arise for discussion are these: (1) Has God really "promised," or are his "promises" really only human hopes? (2) Were the Hebrews, and are we, in a covenant-relationship with God? (3) How does the Old Testament set forth the dilemma with which the doctrine of our redemption must deal? (4) Is Christianity a new religion? What is the relation of the Christian Church to the Hebrew Church? (5) What would a Hebrew Christian understand by the titles given to our Lord in the New Testament? (6) In what sense did prophets and patriarchs foresee Christ? (7) In particular, does the Old Testament predict the Cross of Christ?

WE read in the *Benedictus* that God "hath visited and hath redeemed his people . . . to perform the mercy promised to our forefathers and to remember his holy covenant; to perform the oath which he sware to our forefather Abraham that he would give us." The New Testament is intimately and essentially connected with the Old; the two testaments give us, as Calvin put it, not two religions but two dispensations of one religion. In these days we have been apt to be apologetic about the Old Testament. We admit that it contains many golden passages of high devotional value, and that it gives the background apart from which the New Testament cannot be properly understood; but in general we think of the Old Testament as the Jewish Scriptures, the New as the Christian Scriptures. But this is an error or modern heresy; the Old Testament belongs to the Gospel itself, and is not merely the preparation for it, and this not merely because Christ is foretold in the Old Testament but also because the Old Testament gives the beginnings of the story of our redemption.

"In the beginning God . . ." and in the end God. The Bible moves from Creation through Redemption to the Consummation. It no sooner records the sin and fall of man than it declares the promise—"it shall bruise thy head, and thou shalt bruise his heel." Man is no sooner fallen than God sets about the work of his redemption, and of this work the Bible, the Old Testament as well as the New, is the record down to the arising and first triumphs of the Christian Church. In the Bible there is much that is human history, human aspiration, even human speculation, but the Bible is the Word of God to us because through this human literature there runs the revelation of the mighty acts of God. The Incarnation of the Son of God is not the first action of God in our redemption, even though it be that which illumines and contains all others.

Thus our doctrine of redemption rests in part on the Old Testament. This may be illustrated—but not adequately or comprehensively stated—under a few heads.

(1) The twin ideas of covenant and promise run as a thread through the older Scriptures. Near the middle of the nineteenth century a young Nonconformist minister lay in Manchester on his death-bed. Those around him asked him, after the intimate fashion of those days, how it fared with his soul. He said he was at peace. They asked him upon what his confidence was

based. He answered, "On oaths and promises and blood." Such language would be strange to us to-day, but it has the true Biblical ring about it. He meant that his assurance rested upon the promises of God in the Old Testament, in "the oath that he sware to our forefather Abraham," and that these promises had not merely been declared in word and commended to faith but had been sealed and confirmed by Christ upon the Cross.

The idea of covenant and promise lay near to the early Fathers, but in later years theology was developed along different lines. The Biblical notion was revived and made dominant in theology by John Calvin, who said that the direct and clearest object of faith is the divine benevolence expressed in the most sure promises of God: "we shall have a complete definition of faith, if we say that it is a steady and certain knowledge of the divine benevolence toward us, which, being founded on the truth of the gratuitous promise in Christ, is both revealed to our minds, and confirmed to our hearts by the Holy Ghost."

Promise is correlative to covenant. In an amusing passage the pagan author Lucian describes the consternation of the gods of Olympus when they discover themselves bereft of worshippers; what will happen to them? what are they, if no one recognizes them? The worshippers might seem as necessary to the gods, as the gods were necessary to the worshippers. In much the same way Chemosh, the god of the Moabites, was bound by nature to his people; their victories were his, and their elimination would mean his disappearance. Such was the typical relationship of tribal, local and civic gods to those who worshipped them. The bond between them was of nature, not of choice. Totally and most significantly different was the relationship between Israel and the Lord their God. This was not of nature but of grace; the people depended on their God, but their God in no sense depended upon them; he had chosen them, and he could reject them; they were bound to him, not by a natural tie, but by a covenant relationship. Jehovah of his own sovereign grace elected Israel: "he found him in a desert land, in the waste, howling wilderness; he led him about, he instructed him, he kept him as the apple of his eye. As an eagle stirreth up her nest, fluttereth over her young, spreadeth abroad her wings, taketh them, beareth them on her wings, so the Lord alone did lead him." The religion of Israel was founded upon grace, upon the covenant which God made with Moses in Sinai.

But a covenant is a two-sided instrument. Its validity depends upon its being kept by both parties to it. Israel did not, perhaps could not, keep the covenant. Jehovah was to be their God, and they were to be his people; but, if they would not have him for their God, if they despised his commandments and turned to idolatry in spite of all that he had done for them, how could they remain his people? And yet should the eternal purpose of Jehovah fail? Already, therefore, we see in the Old Testament that tension between the freedom of man to sin and the purpose of God that he shall not sin. The old covenant was a failure. God had done his part, but man had not done his; Israel was free, and Israel would not be the people of God; yet it was God's eternal purpose to choose Israel for himself, and how should God be thwarted? It was an impasse, as the prophets saw it. Therefore, as one of them declared, "behold the days come, saith the Lord, that I will make a new covenant with the house of Israel and with the house of Judah, not according to the covenant that I made with their fathers in the day that I took them by the hand to bring them out of the land of Egypt; which my covenant they brake, although I was an husband unto them, saith the Lord. But this shall be the covenant that I shall make. . . . I will put my law in their inward parts, and write it in their hearts . . . for I will forgive their iniquity, and I will remember their sin no more." This was the faith of a prophet who could see no intellectual solution of the problem. The Ethiopian could as readily change his own skin or the leopard his spots as Israel could walk faithfully with God. Therefore there must be a miracle, and God must create a new heart in his people. But this would be one of the miracles that could not happen; for only by destroying man's freedom, it would seem, could God create a new heart in his people; yet apart from their free consent they could not be his people. That is for all time the setting of the problem of the Atonement.

In the Old Testament it can find no fully satisfactory answer; the answer comes in the New: "this cup is the new covenant in my blood." Redemption is to be understood in terms of covenant.

(2) The Old Testament is concerned with the redemption not only of Israel but also of mankind. It was for the sake of the world that Israel was chosen. We have grown accustomed to speak of a progressive revelation in the Bible; we love to trace the development of religious ideas from the crudities of early Hebrew theology to the sublimity of the New Testament. This as an exercise in human history is legitimate enough. But the Old Testament is concerned less with what man thought than with what God did. God saved Noah, he called Abraham, he destroyed the Egyptians in the Red Sea; he sent his prophets; he raised up Cyrus; in the end he sent his Son. The Old Testament is part of the Gospel because it records the first part of the story of man's redemption. It is true that, if a man believes in Christ, it does not greatly matter if he be ignorant of Abraham or even suppose that he never existed; it is the end, the culmination, of the story that matters most, but the end presupposes the beginning, and of this beginning the Old Testament is the record. The end is that in Abraham shall all the nations of the earth be blessed.

(3) How far back can we trace the history of the Church? To-day we should be disposed to say to Pentecost or to the Resurrection or perhaps to the gathering of the disciples. But the early Fathers knew better. The more mystical or Platonic of them were disposed to say that the Church was created before the moon and the stars, since that which is eternally willed by God has its eternal pattern in the heavens. But the more historically-minded would tell us that the Church begins with the call of Abraham. God called the father of the faithful that he might make of him a great nation, and that in him "all the peoples of the earth" should be blessed. The Old Testament, no less than the Acts of the Apostles, is the story of the Church; the Church is the first-fruits of redemption.

Much of the theology of the Old Testament can be gathered round the notion of the Remnant. The Hebrews as a whole proved "stiff-necked" and rebellious, but, said Isaiah (giving this conviction as a name to his young son), "Remnant shall turn back." Jeremiah appealed again and again to those who were left in northern Israel to "turn back." Ezekiel in exile set himself to build up the faithful remnant and to prepare them for their future task. The seer Daniel has a vision of the ancient empires, represented by a monstrous image, broken in pieces by "a stone cut out without hands," that is, by the faithful, persecuted remnant in Israel. He saw this little stone grow and grow till it filled the whole earth. This may be called the first vision of the universal Church. But before the remnant could cover the whole earth it must first be brought to the lowest straits; it must be represented by One single Figure moving to Jerusalem in majestic preoccupation while his disciples squabble as to who shall be greatest in the Kingdom.

(4) In this connection it may be significant that most of the titles borne by our Lord in the New Testament are patient of a corporate interpretation. Thus the "Son of Man" in Daniel represents "the saints of the Most High"; the "Son of God" is originally Israel—"out of Egypt have I called my Son"; the Servant of the Lord who bears the sins of many is, in Isaiah, at least sometimes, a corporate figure; Messiah, or "anointed one" may be applied to Israel. This suggests not that our Lord is one amongst many brethren but that he is the archetypal Man, the heavenly Man, the representative of the redeemed humanity as is Adam of fallen man; he is the Head of the Church, the Captain of our salvation.

(5) The Gospel, said St. Augustine, lies hid in the Old Testament. The patriarchs and prophets, as the Fathers taught, were already Christians in some forward-looking and proleptic way. The Old Testament is a story the meaning of which is not revealed till we reach the end; it is only to be understood in the light of that which came out of it. For this reason much of the Biblical criticism of the past few generations, though invaluable from the point of view of history and scholarship, is beside the mark as concerns Christian theology. In the old days, for instance, it was confidently believed by our fathers that Abraham and Moses and Isaiah and many of the saints of

the Old Testament foresaw the coming of Christ and even predicted the events of his life. Modern scholars have vehemently denied this and have interpreted the so-called Messianic predictions in terms of the political situation of the writer's day or the limited religious notions of his time. There is truth in both these views, but we shall be wise to start from the interpretations of modern scholars. We can no longer think that the map of the future lay open before the prophets, and that they could foresee, for instance, the flight into Egypt, the birth of Christ at Bethlehem of the Virgin Mary or the parting of his garments among the soldiers round the Cross. On the other hand, we may not limit the prophet's vision to a literal and exact and purely contemporary interpretation of his words. The language of a poet or prophet is always and necessarily inadequate to his thought. When the prophet speaks of the eternal purposes of God, he declares that which he cannot photographically foresee but dimly yet surely apprehends: "I shall see him, but not now," said Balaam, "I shall behold him but not nigh; there shall come a Star out of Jacob, and a Sceptre shall rise out of Israel, and shall smite the corners of Moab, and destroy all the children of Sheth." Balaam declares the coming redemption. True, he sees it in terms of the tribal superiority of the Hebrews, for how could he, in that age, see it in other terms? But God answers our prayers not according to the limitations of our vision or our expectation but according to his "how much more"! The prophets of the Old Testament did not consciously and, as it were, pictorially foresee Christ, but they declared the redemption which God would work, they foresaw that which, beyond their realization, meant the Incarnation of the Son of God. The prophets saw "through a glass darkly"—but they saw. Their theology was inadequate to the reality which God in the fulness of time revealed, and we may be sure that our own stumbling theological efforts still fall far short of those things "which for our unworthiness we dare not, and for our blindness we cannot, ask."

This is not to suggest that in respect of our redemption we may be indefinite and vague, but it is a reminder of the true Agnosticism which recognizes in humility and wonder that

God's thoughts are not as our thoughts, neither are his ways our ways. It is true that we Christians have a definite creed, while the saints of the Old Church had none, but a creed which is the starting-point for faith and love serves us ill if it lead us to think we have the answer to all questions and the final truth. We can see farther into the mystery of our redemption than the Old Church could; prophets and kings desired to see the things which we have seen. But, if we have seen much, we have not seen all: "brethren, now are we the children of God, and it doth not yet appear what we shall be." At best our theology is, as they used to say, *theologia viae*, not *theologia patriae*, a theology of pilgrims on their way, not the final theology of our heavenly fatherland, when we shall know even as we are known.

(6) Outstanding in the religion of the Old Testament are the so-called Songs of the Servant of the Lord, particularly Isaiah xlii. 1–4, xlix. 1–6, l. 4–9, lii. 15–liii. 12. Elsewhere the Old Testament looks forward to a Messiah who shall be "great David's greater Son," the conqueror who shall inherit the nations, ruling them with a rod of iron and breaking them in pieces like a potter's vessel. But in these passages of Isaiah we find prediction of a very different sort of person, one, indeed, who "is despised and rejected of men, a man of sorrows and acquainted with grief"; of him it is said, "surely he hath borne our griefs and carried our sorrows. . . . He was wounded for our transgressions, he was bruised for our iniquities, the chastisement of our peace was upon him, and with his stripes we are healed . . . he hath poured out his soul unto death; and he was numbered with the transgressors; and he bare the sin of many, and made intercession for the transgressors." It is inevitable that Christian readers think of Christ; but did the inspired writer really foresee the Crucifixion? Modern scholars are divided about this passage. Some say that the poet had in mind a particular heroic figure—Moses, perhaps, or Hosea, or Jeremiah; others say that the Servant is an ideal or imaginary figure; others interpret the Servant as Israel or the faithful remnant. This is a problem of scholarship which may find no solution while time lasts. But we Christians rightly say that the prophet has foreseen

Christ, for he has had a glimpse into heavenly and spiritual principles and truths which inevitably point to Christ.

The covenant made at Sinai was broken; God must make a new covenant with man and create a clean heart in him that he may keep it; but how could God do that without violence to man's freedom? This chapter in Isaiah suggests that men may be changed with their own consent as they see one who voluntarily suffers for their sins and gives himself to death in love for them; yes, such an one would see of the travail of his soul and would be satisfied. Can even we after Calvary see more deeply into the mystery?

It may seem strange that in this chapter on the Old Testament nothing has been said about the Day of Atonement and the sacrificial system. Some recompense will be made in the next chapter; meanwhile it is important to remember that one term like "sacrifice" cannot cover all the mystery. Enough of it has been indicated that the Old Testament gives the first instalment of the Gospel of our redemption.

CHAPTER III

The New Testament Fulfilment

The New Testament describes our Redemption in many metaphors and varied terms. Some of these are here considered. Redemption is considered first as the remission of a debt, second as delivery from slavery; then it is related to the idea of "the Kingdom of God." Next an attempt is made to explain the sacrificial terminology of the New Testament. Some of St. Paul's terms are explained—"propitiation," "justification." What, we ask finally, is our redemption from the point of view of God himself? Redemption is personal reconciliation with our heavenly Father.

The following books may be suggested for further reading: (1) *Christ and His Cross*, by W. R. Maltby (Epworth Press); (2) *A Man in Christ*, by J. Stewart (Hodder & Stoughton); (3) *The Gospel in the New Testament*, by C. H. Dodd (National Sunday School Union); (4) *The Apostolic Preaching*, by C. H. Dodd (Hodder & Stoughton).

Questions that arise for discussion are such as these: (1) In what sense can sin be called a debt or an enslavement? (2) What is to be understood by "the Kingdom of God"? (3) What exactly is meant by "salvation by the blood of Christ"? (4) In what sense is Christ the "propitiation for our sins"? (5) What is "justification by faith"? (6) Does the Parable of the Prodigal Son suggest salvation without the Cross of Christ? (7) What would it mean to be reconciled with God?

THE New Testament is concerned with redemption from the first page to the last. The notion is expressed and indicated and illustrated by a bewildering variety of metaphors and symbols. That we may understand what has happened to men, or may happen to them, through the work of Christ, it will be convenient briefly to note some typical expressions.

(1) We may start from the familiar metaphor debt. It is derived from the teaching of our Lord himself. He depicts a debtor coming to his creditor and begging to be let off, for he cannot pay; the creditor "was moved with compassion and loosed him and forgave him the debt." Such, we are to understand, is the attitude of God to us, provided only that we forgive

our debtors. To be in debt, to be unable to pay, to see all future days pledged to the impossible task of repayment, to realize that there can be no deliverance from this bondage while life last, to approach the creditor, to plead for mercy, to hear him say, "You cannot pay? Well, do you think a thing like that is going to stand between you and me? Say no more about the debt"—such-like is our redemption. But to understand the force of the image, we must have come to the point where we have felt our sins to have been strangling us, slowly, relentlessly, endlessly like an unpayable and ever-mounting debt.

The image taken from debt is vivid and compelling, but it will not serve as the sole basis for a theology of the Atonement. Some theologians have sought to show that Christ paid our debt for us, as if sin could be adequately described as the incurring of a debt, but sin, as our own hearts tell us, is more inward and personal than that. Others with an eye to this metaphor have made light of sin, as if there were no need for the Cross, the creditor in the parable remitting the debt without thought of any recompense; but, once again, sin is a perversion of the personality; it must be destroyed; God, who is true and righteous, cannot say of it, like the creditor in the parable, "do not mention it, it is nothing between you and me." The remission of debt, then, is a metaphor, not a theology, of our redemption.

(2) This word "redemption" is itself a metaphor. It looks to the bitterness of slavery. When it was first used, the world was familiar with the slave-market; human beings were bought and sold as chattels without rights of their own; their personal affections or desires were not considered for a moment. This nightmare has largely passed from the world. As we are well aware, we have not yet attained economic freedom for all men, but political freedom is no little thing, and the rights of man as man are, except under totalitarian forms of government, now recognized. But, as I write, there are hundreds of thousands of men in Europe in captivity, virtual or actual, torn from their homes, set to work for their masters and treated as less than human. We can dimly imagine what it would mean to one such man to be told in the morning, "you can go home to-day, you are free for ever." It was an experience like that which

the early Christians had in mind when they said that they had been "redeemed" by Christ.

Readers of Dickens will have a vivid sense of the debtors' prison where men languished for years without hope of freedom unless some good friend could be found to buy them out. In the ancient world, similarly, a slave must remain a slave knowing that his freedom could be bought for money usually far beyond his utmost means. "The Son of Man came . . . to give his life a ransom for many." We were like the hopeless debtor, like the desperate slave till we were "ransomed" by the death of Christ. Our first need is not for a satisfactory theology of our redemption but for a feeling sense of that from which at such cost Christ has brought us free. Our senses and our spiritual perceptions are too dim for us to have at present any adequate "theology" of the redemption; we must first stand with the early Christians like men who know at last that they are free after an intolerable and once hopeless bondage.

(3) The teaching of our Lord is largely in terms of "the Kingdom of God." According to the Jewish thought of his time this present age was subject to Satan and the powers of darkness represented by the dominance of the heathen Roman empire. One day God would destroy this age and usher in the days of the Messiah or the Kingdom of God. Our Lord taught that in his own mission and person the Kingdom of God was already here on earth. This Kingdom was a new world in which men could live now, and the Christians knew themselves to be those who had been "translated out of darkness into the Kingdom of his dear Son." To understand this, we should not, in the first instance, study works of theology but try to find out from Jews or other refugees from Nazi Germany what it meant to them to find themselves at last in a country that is free. Even those, who have only travelled in Nazi Germany, may remember the thankfulness, the relief, the elation with which they stepped from under the loathed swastika flag back on to English soil. Perhaps we have to be brought clean out of utter heathenism fully to appreciate what is meant by the Kingdom of God, that world, that sphere, that company where God reigns and his ways are loved.

It was often said in earlier days that the Christian life begins with the conviction of sin. This sometimes led to unnatural attempts to produce a sense of sin and occasionally even to pathological religious states. Yet the three metaphors so far considered—from debt, from slavery and from the idea of a kingdom—can only be understood as we have an ever deeper sense of that from which by God's grace we have been delivered.

(4) "The Son of man came . . . to give his life"; "Christ our Passover is sacrificed for us"; "behold, the Lamb of God that taketh away the sin of the world"; "ye were not redeemed with corruptible things . . but with the precious blood of Christ as of a lamb without blemish and without spot." Again and again throughout the New Testament the death of Christ is interpreted or illustrated in terms of sacrifice. The language of sacrifice has been taken up into Christian worship, but it has largely lost its radiance. In our ordinary speech to sacrifice means voluntarily to give up; the ancient sacrificial system of the Old Testament has become for us emotionally and theoretically unintelligible; we see nothing sacred in the slaughtering of animals—rather the reverse—and our offerings in kind for the Harvest Festival are not usually fraught with deep religious feeling. We cannot easily imagine the mental state of those who in the great moments of life have felt constrained to kill something in order to come into the right relationship with God. Sacrifice whether of animals or fruits, which in the ancient world was common and an obvious duty, has been unknown amongst us for a thousand years and more; it has lost its meaning. Therefore it is imperatively necessary that we find other terms in which to express to our contemporaries the work of Christ. Yet, if we are to read our Bibles intelligently we must have some idea of the intellectual and emotional tone of this sacrificial language in the New Testament.

One of our difficulties here is that, while sacrifice is mentioned and presupposed throughout the Bible, it is always assumed and never explained. There is in the Bible no theory or theology of sacrifice, and we may be sure that in different periods and according to different degrees of religious insight men's thoughts about sacrifice varied widely. We may see crowds on a holiday afternoon going to put flowers by the graves in a great cemetery. Few of those who do this have a theory of why they do it; it is a token of love; it seems "the natural thing to do"; it is a custom which in some obscure way corresponds with an emotional or spiritual impulse; it is not a matter of theory or speculation. So with sacrifice in the ancient world. But we should certainly put from our minds any thought that in the New Testament or amongst the spiritually-minded Jews crude thoughts were associated with sacrifice, as if, for instance, they thought God should be bribed, or that God had any need of these material gifts or pleasure in them as material things. Professor Vincent Taylor suggests that

> the true significance of the sacrificial element in New Testament teaching is to be found, not so much in the specific rites of the cultus, as in the underlying ideas of sacrifice, the idea of the drawing near of the worshipper to God in humility and contrition, the thought of an offering with which he can identify himself in penitence and faith, the conception of sharing in the cleansing power of life which has been released in death, dedicated and presented to God. It is not simply a matter of separate ideas, but of a religious standpoint, a group of religious assumptions bearing upon the problem of the renewal of a fellowship broken by sin.

Perhaps these ideas, in part at least, are not so remote from us as at first sight we suppose. This may be indicated by a trivial illustration: you have quarrelled with a friend and are estranged; words were used which cannot very easily be forgotten or taken back. It is a wretched situation, but there you are—estranged. There comes a knock on the door, and there is the florist with a bunch of flowers and your friend's card attached to them. Will you accept them or reject them? Observe that this is not just a simple question whether you like those particular flowers, or whether you have the right vase in which to place them. You are presented with a psychological or, rather, with a spiritual problem. Those are not just blossoms; they are also a message, a symbol; they are a plea for reconciliation. You can refuse the parcel; but, if you do that, you have done much more than given the florist the chance of selling the flowers again; you have struck your friend a blow. Or, if you receive the flowers, you must do more than put them in a vase; you must return thanks for them; you must get into touch with your friend again; you must be reconciled. This is obvious enough, but it takes us far into the ancient thought of sacrifice. The Hebrew felt himself estranged from God by sin; how was he to be reconciled with God? God in his mercy had provided a way: if he would bring God the appointed gift and offer it with penitence, God would accept it. God would accept the gift and not reject the giver.

Some of the Hebrew sacrifices were of a joyful kind, such as the offering of the first-fruits. We may make just such a sacrifice to God when we are allowed to give the flowers for the Communion Table. But where sin was involved, there must be a mood of penitence, not joy, and the sacrifice usually entailed the victim's death. For those of us who are city dwellers it is difficult to appreciate the emotional tension that went with the sacrifice of life. But it is not necessary that we understand this, for we are well aware that

> Not all the blood of beasts
>   On Jewish altars slain
> Could give the guilty conscience peace,
>   Or wash away the stain.

What, then, shall we offer to God, that we may be reconciled, we that are estranged from him by sin? In the most solemn rite of the Christian religion we come before him with our offering which he has promised to accept. It is nothing of our own that we can offer; we can but plead Christ who is both our sacrifice and our High Priest. He has identified himself with us; he has called us his brethren; he, the eternal Son of God, has passed through Calvary for us, and risen again for us, and now

> Entered the holy place above,
>   Covered with meritorious scars,
> The tokens of his dying love,
>   Our great High Priest in glory bears.
> He pleads his Passion on the Tree,
> He shows himself to God for me.

It is very proper, therefore, that the Mass or Communion Service should be spoken of in terms of sacrifice, not, indeed, that we think there to repeat the sacrifice that was made "once for all" on Calvary, but because there we identify ourselves by desire and love with the eternal sacrifice of Christ, which is dramatically and sacramentally set forth, and there we receive the tokens of our acceptance for his sake.

Not only the older form of evangelism but every type of Biblical Christianity speaks of our salvation "by the blood of Christ." This phrase is a stumbling-block to many in these days. This is partly due to traditional forms of theology which, understood or misunderstood, have offended the moral sense of modern men, and partly to sheer misunderstanding of the sacrificial language of the New Testament. It seems that in the ancient animal-sacrifices the most significant moment was not the death of the victim, but the application of its blood to the worshipper. The blood is the life, as the Old Testament puts it in one of its few comments upon sacrifice. The blood of the victim is the life that has passed through death. When, therefore, we say that we are saved "by the blood of Christ," we are ascribing our salvation, not to the death of Christ nor to some mysterious transaction on Calvary, but to the life of Christ, the life that has passed through death. The phrase means simply, we are saved by the living One who was crucified. That is a statement of simple fact.

(5) The doctrine of our redemption owes much to the letters of the Apostle Paul. Some of his words need interpretation for our days, in particular, the word "propitiation" as used in our accepted versions. He speaks of Christ "whom God hath set forth to be a propitiation through faith in his blood." This naturally and inevitably suggests to us that in some way Christ on the Cross propitiates an angry God, and we are wont to forget that, even if this were the meaning of "propitiation" here, it is God who initiates it on our behalf. The gods of the pagan world had to be propitiated by their worshippers, and the verbal form of the word here used by St. Paul was used by the pagans in that sense, but in the Greek Bible the word has an almost opposite sense; there it means the performance of an

act whereby guilt or defilement is removed. In accordance with Biblical usage, therefore, says Professor C. H. Dodd, the word means not propitiation but a means by which guilt is annulled:

> the rendering "propitiation" is therefore misleading, for it suggests the placating of an angry God, and although this would be in accord with pagan usage, it is foreign to Biblical usage. In the present passage it is God who "puts forward the means" whereby the guilt of sin is removed, by sending Christ. The sending of Christ, therefore, is the divine method of forgiveness.

(6) Another Pauline term that needs elucidation is "justification." We are "justified," he says, by faith. This is first and foremost a metaphor taken from the law-courts. When a man after standing trial is dismissed "without a stain upon his character," he is "justified." In other words, he is acquitted. "We must all stand before the judgment-seat of Christ"; there is, therefore, a basis for the expression of our redemption in terms of the courts. In the Last Day at the Great Assize believers will be acquitted. But Christ is not only our Judge, he is also our Saviour, our Brother, our High Priest, the Captain of our salvation. Metaphors taken from the law-courts can never be adequate to our relations with our Lord, who deals with us, not on a legal basis, but in grace. And, as a matter of fact, this word "justified," while it means "acquitted," means much more in its connotations and associations. Our terms "just," "justice," "justify," "righteous" and "righteousness" are all covered by a single root in Greek. Professor Dodd has shown that in the meaning of the Bible "righteousness" in God is not, as it were, a passive quality but an outgoing energy; God vindicates his righteousness by making it prevail, he "openly declares his righteousness in the sight of the heathen" by the extension of his holy rule. This "justification" in the Hebrew Bible means "an act by which a wronged person is given his rights, is vindicated, delivered from oppression." Thus, when God is said to "justify the ungodly," this means, not, as modern usage might suggest, that he condones their ungodliness nor even that he deems them to be godly, but

rather that he delivers them from the bondage of ungodliness. Thus "justification" in St. Paul's letters connotes the deliverance of God, whereby God frees man from the power of the enemy and so claims him for his own. "Justification," then, means "acquittal," but even more it means "deliverance." This, therefore, is one of the terms in the New Testament which provides a basis for those later theologies which have interpreted the work of Christ primarily in terms of victory over the enemy of souls.

(7) Our redemption, then, means that we are as debtors whose debt is cancelled, as slaves set free, as those translated into a new world under a new ruler, as those reconciled to God by sacrifice, as those for whom God has provided pardon and deliverance. This is what our redemption means to us. Can we say what it means to God? This is suggested to us in three parables which in our Bibles are placed side by side, the parable of the lost sheep, of the lost coin, and of the lost son. The shepherd weary at the end of the day finds that one sheep is missing from the flock; out he goes, straight away, over the rocky hills in the dark looking for that one lost sheep "until he find," and when he finds it, what rejoicing! A poor woman has lost a sixpence; it is not much, but it is all she has; she sweeps out her whole house, which is but a single room, and when the lost coin is found, even the neighbours must join in the celebration. A father has lost his wastrel son, who has come to grief and found himself in the gutter; but when he is yet a long way off, his father runs to meet him and falls on his neck and kisses him. Our Lord indicates that such is the love and yearning of our God for us. The undiscerning have said that there is no Cross in the story of the Prodigal Son; therefore the forgiveness of God is a simple thing requiring no Calvary and no mediation. But parents will know better.

(8) A scholar, intimately familiar with all the records of pagan mysticism and mystery religions in these early centuries has claimed that for most of the terms in the New Testament he can find some sort of parallel elsewhere. Pagans could conceive that their gods might bring them out of bondage or remit

their debts, but paganism never dreamed that God could be "reconciled" to man. Our redemption means, first and last, that we are pardoned and reconciled with God; it is a personal relationship; its cost to God is measured by the Cross. It is the immeasurable, inconceivable mystery and abyss of grace.

CHAPTER IV

The Saviour of the World

Many passages in the New Testament point to a cosmic or universal salvation wrought by our Lord. How is he to be conceived as the Saviour of all men if, as many other passages indicate, some are lost? This issue is the more urgent to-day because convinced Christians are in a great minority, yet are bound by ties of affection and respect to great numbers who are outside the Church. We must, therefore, consider afresh the doctrine of the Fathers that Christ becomes the Saviour of humanity by assuming our common human nature. There is, or there may be, human solidarity "in Christ," as all men are one "in Adam."

Historic doctrines of our redemption may be briefly and conveniently studied in *The Doctrine of the Work of Christ*, by S. Cave (London Theological Library). On the subject of this chapter Mrs. Gorodetzki's *The Humiliated Christ in Modern Russian Thought* (S.P.C.K.) is to be commended.

Questions for discussion are: (1) How should we understand the New Testament teaching that the whole universe is to be gathered up in Christ? (2) Should we think of the Incarnation as God's remedy for sin or as the original purpose of Creation? (3) Can we reconcile the New Testament teaching about "hell" with the idea that Christ is the Saviour of all men? (4) Does redemption involve personal response on our part? (5) In what sense is humanity one "in Adam"? Is this idea of human solidarity applicable in the sphere of religion?

I

REDEMPTION is reconciliation to God. What, then, or who, are the subject of reconciliation? So far, redemption has for the most part been described in terms of the sense of deliverance felt by the individual who knows himself redeemed. But are we only redeemed if we feel ourselves to be delivered, and if we have enjoyed some religious experience akin to that which lies behind these triumphant metaphors of the New Testament? Is it only the few, the very few, who are redeemed?

It pleased the Father, says the Apostle, that in Christ "should all the fulness dwell; and, having made peace through the blood of his Cross, by him to reconcile all things unto himself; by him, I say, whether they be things in earth or things in heaven." In other words, it seemed good to God that by the blood of the Cross the whole universe should be reconciled to God. Similarly, "the mystery of God's will" is defined as his purpose "to gather together in one all things in Christ, both which are in heaven, and which are on earth." The word here translated "gather together" means originally to "sum up," as an orator sums up his speech. The whole universe, then, visible and invisible, is to be gathered together and summed up in Christ. The universe is, as it were, a vast and intricate canvas with one central Figure who gives meaning to the whole; that Figure is Christ. The place of Christ in the whole scheme of things, then, far exceeds that of being the Saviour only of the few "elect."

Milton's *Paradise Lost* and Bunyan's *Holy War* have done much to accustom us to the idea that the Incarnation of the Son of God was, as it were, God's afterthought, his remedy for sin, no part of his original intention. But there have been theologians like Duns Scotus who have taught, not without some Scriptural warrant, that the Incarnation of the Son was the very purpose and meaning of Creation; "all things were created by him and for him"; his Passion, no doubt, was due to sin, but his Coming to manifest the glory of God in human form was that for which the world was made. Such speculation is too high for us, and, besides, it would deflect us from the smaller problem of our own redemption. Yet these passages which indicate the cosmic significance of Christ are important for our present purpose because they indicate a work for the whole of humanity, and not for the few alone. Thus, in the Gospel of St. John the Samaritans say of our Lord that "we know that this is indeed the Christ, the Saviour of the World," and the Baptist hails the Messiah as "the Lamb of God which taketh away the sin of the world." Are we to understand that in the end all the world with every one in it is to be saved, that the redemption wrought by Christ is universal in its efficacy?

We may be sure that we are wrong if we think we see a simple and clear answer to this question. The idea that our Lord really is the Saviour of the whole world, not merely by desire but also in fact, crops up again and again throughout the history of Christian thought, but rarely or never has it been made dominant in theology. The Church, it would seem, has built rather on the text that "many are called, but few are chosen," and there has been a crop of unconvincing speculations as to the number of the elect. Christ, it has been often supposed, could have saved everybody, for his sacrifice sufficed to wipe out the sins of the whole world; but in fact God in his inscrutable Providence has been willing to save only a limited number. Thus saintly theologians like St. Anselm have argued that it is just that God should punish the guilty, for they are guilty; it is just that he should spare other guilty for Christ's sake, for in the end whatever God wills is just, and there is no more that we can say about it.

If a man had unlimited money for the payment of his friends' debts and should rescue only a few of them from the debtors' prison, leaving the rest to languish there, we should not be impressed by his goodness or his mercy, and we may be very sure that any theology has gone grievously astray which in effect gives such a picture of the purposes of God. On the other hand, those who in recent generations have proclaimed that the kindness of God will inevitably insure the eternal blessedness of everybody have not greatly impressed religious men; for, in the first place, if certain texts in the Bible have seemed to support this view, many more seem as clearly to contradict it, and, in the second, this notion has seemed to lack moral seriousness and to be too reminiscent of the Rubaiyat:

> Folk of a surly Tapster tell
> And daub his visage with the smoke of hell;
> They talk of some strict testing of us—Pish!
> He's a good fellow, and 'twill all be well.

God, as he is represented in the Holy Scriptures, is not like Omar's "good fellow"; on the other hand, he cannot will the death of a sinner but rather would have all men saved; therefore, so far as it lies with God, our salvation is sure. Christ will save all whom he can save. Are there, then, limits to the power, as there are none to the grace, of God?

We are bound to raise these questions; we are bound to be baffled by them. The easy way out is, as always, to refuse to see both sides, to take the view that God is kind, therefore all will be well for everybody, or the view that God is inscrutable, and we must just take it that all unbelievers will be damned. There can be little doubt that, if traditional orthodoxy is rather on the side of the latter view, the former is much nearer to the insights of our age. We may fairly say that the notions of redemption with which we have grown to be familiar in Church do not seem to give any very satisfactory meaning to the teaching of the Bible that Christ is the Saviour of the whole world, or that it is the purpose of God to reconcile to himself all things, and therefore all persons, by the blood of the Cross. It is right, therefore, that we should pay special attention to this more neglected side of the teaching of the Scriptures.

II

In the last two generations there has been amongst us a great increase of humanitarian feeling, amounting, sometimes, to a weak sentimentalism. At the same time there has come a decrease in our moral earnestness and depth. We do not take sin so seriously or tragically as our fathers did; we tend to explain it away as "growing pains" or the result of heredity or the product of environment; we have been psycho-analysed and are disposed in our charity to ascribe to "complexes" what other generations called rebellion against God. It has therefore not seemed too much to ask of God that he should overlook the regrettable incidents in which we have unfortunately become involved, and all this talk about the necessity of Calvary for forgiveness and of salvation "by the blood of Jesus" has sounded utterly remote and meaningless. Our redemption, from this complacent point of view, is the process by which we "let the ape and tiger die" within us, the evolutionary progress from the mud to the stars. It need scarcely be said that this superficial and sentimental temper of mind is wholly alien to Biblical religion; it is not the Christian faith. Nothing of this sort is indicated when our Lord is called the Saviour of the world.

"O Saviour of the world, the Son Lord Jesus, who by thy Cross and precious blood hast redeemed us, save us and help us, we humbly beseech thee"—so begins an ancient "sequence." If Christ is the Saviour of all the world, it is in virtue of his Cross. How can we understand this? We are disposed to say that, if redemption implies conscious response on our part, Christ is not the Redeemer of those who make no response to him; if, on the other hand, redemption does not involve conscious response, it must be something mechanical, impersonal, "magical." Is there a way out of this dilemma?

As was hinted in the introductory chapter, this question has become increasingly urgent in these days. There was a time in Europe when all one's friends were baptized, and it was reasonable to hope that they were within the covenant of grace; the question of the salvability of the heathen was not acutely felt. The Book of Common Prayer contains a collect for Jews, Turks, infidels and heretics, but a concern for "those outside" is not a dominant *motif* of any liturgy. But in these days both of secularism and of national solidarity in suffering and endeavour, it is, and it ought to be, almost impossible for us to think of redemption in purely individual terms. Those of us who survive this war will owe an immeasurable and unrepayable debt to countless men and women who, believers and unbelievers alike, will have suffered and died for us and those like us. Is it really to be thought that we should be content to enjoy "heaven" without a thought for the fate of these? If we feel like that about our social solidarity with our fellows, we may be sure that our dim love for them is but a very pale reflection of the love of Christ. This is but a special instance of a general principle. We are not merely individuals; we are also persons, and a person is constituted in part by his relation to other persons. Those whom we love dwell in our hearts; to cut them out of our thought would be to cut out part of ourselves; our happiness is bound up with theirs; we might even dare to say that heaven would not be heaven for us, if we knew that they were excluded from it. And in all such arguments from our own affections we are bound to say, "How much more Christ!" For these reasons we are called to-day to ponder the declaration of the Gospel that Christ is the Saviour of the world.

The traditional theologies of the Cross with which we are familiar throw little light upon this pressing question. It is likely that, if we are to find some answer that will meet our present need, we must turn back to the early Fathers of the Church, to St. Irenaeus and those who followed his lead.

III

We are saved "by the blood of Jesus," but, as we have seen, the "blood" of Jesus means his life; we are saved by the life of him who for us was crucified. We may not rightly separate his death from his birth on the one side and, on the other, from his resurrection and continual presence with his people. We are saved by the Incarnate Lord. The ground of our salvation, then, is the Incarnation. Our Lord "took our nature upon him." The early Church, especially in the East, made this conception basic for its theology. We cannot immediately and easily translate its theology into modern terms, but we may hope to find here hints and suggestions which will help us.

The thought of the early Fathers may be put like this: all human beings share in common that which is called human nature. This human nature is constituted by a human body, a human mind, a human soul or, as we might put it, a human psycho-physical organism. This human nature is identical in all men. But all men are distinguished from each other by their individuality. Thus Peter and James and John are distinct in respect of their personal and individual peculiarities, but they share the same human nature. This human nature was not conceived as an extended, solid substance of which each individual possessed a little bit. Rather, being common to all men it was wholly possessed by each. We might perhaps illustrate this from the life in the human body, which is possessed wholly by each part of the body. This life is not a substance such that if, for instance, we cut off our living hairs, there is less life in us than there was before; our whole life is wholly in every part of our body while it is alive; thus in one part it is the life of a toe, in another part of a finger, in another part of the heart; yet it is the same, single life everywhere. This may not be a strictly scientific illustration, but it shows how we easily conceive that which is not material as being wholly "in several places at once." Human nature was conceived in that fashion. There was not more human nature when some new child was born, not less when some one died, but each living person possessed that human nature which was present in all human beings as a man's physical life is present in each part of his living body. All men are one, one body, in Adam, that is, in respect of their human nature. But now in Christ God has united human nature, that is, humanity, with himself, that as in Adam all die, even so in Christ should all be made alive. That human nature in which we all share has been lifted up to heaven and joined to God.

From a different aspect we might say that humanity is a body which is sick throughout and diseased. When Christ took our human nature upon him, it meant that at one point into this diseased body of humanity there had been injected that which was wholly healthy. This did not imply that immediately the whole body would recover health, but only that health was now available for every part, for the whole body shares in the life of every part.

This must not be taken as a careful analysis or as scientific exegesis of the theology of St. Irenaeus or of any other of the Fathers, but only as an indication of the kind of way in which they regarded the Incarnation as the saving work of Christ through the taking of the human nature which is common to humanity. It has been objected that such a notion of human nature is philosophically unsatisfactory, and that the whole circle of ideas is physical, not spiritual. But it should not be impossible to translate these ideas into personal and non-physical terms, and, if we do so, it is probable that we are much nearer to the real meaning of the Fathers than if we interpret their language too literally and prosaically.

Professor Victor Murray of Hull once described a visit of inspection which he had paid to a local school. The headmaster, being busy, deputed a small boy to show him round the buildings. The boy he chose was small and grubby and not prone to use his pocket-handkerchief; in fact, he was at first sight definitely unattractive. However, he rose to the occasion as best he could, and acted as a competent showman. When he came to the hall, he pointed to the commemorative boards, and said, "you know, Sir, we have a general and two Cabinet ministers from this school." Presently he added, "and you know, Sir, we have won all our matches this term!" "Are you in the team, then?" asked Mr. Murray. "Oh no, Sir, of course I'm not," answered the boy. Then he said shyly, "you know, Sir, you must not judge the school by me." "We won all our matches . . . you must not judge the school by me"—it was not just the team that won the matches, it was the school. The school consists only of individuals, but the whole school shares in the triumphs or failures of its representatives. As with a school, so with a nation. We won the battle of Waterloo, we brought the troops back from Dunkirk, we bombed Augsburg. In what sense did "we" do these things, we who were born long after Waterloo, we who have never been to sea or ridden the air in a bomber? It may be very difficult to give a philosophical answer to this question, but we all know as a matter of intuition and experience that there is such a thing as corporate life in which the achievements of each are in some real sense the achievements of all.

Humanity through the ages is such another corporate life in the failures and achievements of which we all participate. We discovered the way to kindle fire, we invented the wheel, we levelled the forests and tilled the ground; we scanned and mapped the stars, we calculated their distances and divined their elements, we have harnessed Nature to our purposes, we have banished slavery—all this we have done. The triumphs of humanity are our triumphs, and, on the other side, the sins, cruelties and devilries of humanity are likewise ours. Our inheritance "in Adam" is an inheritance of shame and misery as well as of achievement. But into this humanity, "made in the image of God" and yet "sold under sin," there has come the Son of God. As our country's victories are ours if we are Britons, so Christ's victories are ours if we are his. What he has done, his Church has done—"we won all our matches . . . you must not judge the school by me." Indeed, Christ's victory is humanity's victory, for, as we are one in Adam, so are we one in him who took on himself our human nature. Thus it was said of Christ that on the Cross with arms outstretched "he took to himself the soul of every man, for better for worse, for richer for poorer, and death never shall us part." We have all sinned and fallen short of the glory of God, and Christ has identified himself with us all, and will never let us go. He has taken our nature upon him; he has made himself one with all humanity; he is the Saviour of the world. The Church is the Body of Christ, but in another sense all humanity is his Body.

This is not a formal theological doctrine; it is an aspect of the mystery of our redemption which is suggested to us by certain passages in Scripture and by a consideration of the teaching of the early Fathers of the Church. It is not "orthodox" or "heretical"; it is a glimpse into the dazzling brightness of the grace of God.

Sometimes the Fathers use language which might seem to suggest that our Lord, by taking our nature, almost automatically saved the whole human race, but this was not their meaning or their thought. The redemption that Christ won for us must be appropriated in the Church by faith and by the sacraments. Nor was the whole of their teaching summed up in this doctrine as I have outlined or suggested it. They interpreted the work of Christ as a victory over Satan, sometimes through a ransom paid to him. But in this chapter we look at one aspect of the matter only.

Christ is the Representative Man, the heavenly Adam, the Head of the redeemed humanity. By taking our human nature upon him, he identified himself with all; it is for all to identify themselves with him by faith and love.

But, if some appropriation of Christ's work by us is necessary, we still have no light upon the significance of his work for those who through lack of opportunity or dullness of perception have in this life made no due response. Here as elsewhere we are prying into mysteries that we cannot fathom, and no final or speculative or theoretical answer is given us, but we are not wholly without light. We cannot claim that the clause in the creed, "he descended into hell", is based upon a consensus of many passages in Scripture, nor that its implications have been carefully worked out in theology; it is one of the clauses which cannot rightly be taken prosaically and literally, for no one supposes that the departed linger in some place below the earth. But it points to a religious apprehension that the work of Christ did not avail only for those who responded to his teaching after the Incarnation. He threw open the gates of everlasting life to all the faithful. In pictorial language he preached to those who died before his Coming, and those who responded he brought with him in his triumph over death. This conception was integral to the faith of the early Church, which was well persuaded that the prophets and patriarchs and martyrs of the Old Testament belonged to the true Church. We may perhaps with all due hesitation extend further the idea. Many are the terrible warnings in Scripture against those who deny and refuse the proffered salvation. Denial, however, is one thing; to have failed to respond through ignorance or dullness is another. We are here beyond our depth, but we may be permitted to consider the lines of the modern poet:

> Some may perchance with strange surprise
> Have blundered into paradise.
> In vasty dusk of life abroad
> They fondly thought to err from God,
> Nor knew the circle that they trod;
> And wandering all the night about
> Found them at morn where they set out.
> Death dawned; heaven lay in prospect wide—
> Lo! they were standing by His side!

CHAPTER V

Christus Victor

St. John of Damascus, from whom several quotations are taken in this chapter, lived from about A.D. 675-749. He was poet and saint and systematic theologian. His great work *On the Orthodox Faith* sums up the early teaching of the Christian Fathers of the East. He was the last of the Eastern Fathers greatly to influence the thought of Western Christianity. He lived and wrote when the "infidels," the Mohammedans, were laying waste the Christian Church. In the last chapter we considered redemption by the Incarnation; we here consider redemption by the Cross understood as the Victory of Christ over all the powers of evil and of darkness. It was fitting that evil should be overcome "in man, for man." The victory of Christ is not a matter of faith unsupported by evidence, for the triumphs of the Cross belong to history. "The Cross" in this connection means not only the historic event on Calvary but also the Word of the Cross proclaimed in preaching or conveyed in sacrament.

Under the title *Christus Victor*, Bishop Aulén of Sweden (S.P.C.K.) has discussed this aspect of the work of Christ. It would be interesting to inquire how the hymnody of the Church in every age and every branch constantly recurs to the *motif* of the victory of Christ.

Questions that arise for discussion are: (1) Has sin really been defeated? (2) Has death really been overcome for us who have to die? (3) What is the distinction between immortality and resurrection? (4) Must we "give the devil his due," and, if so, what is his due? (5) Is the success of Christian missions a proof of the truth of the Christian faith? (6) What is the relation between Calvary and "the sacrament of the altar"? (7) What is the difference between preaching and instruction?

IN the last chapter we considered chiefly that aspect of our redemption which was expressed in the doctrine of the Fathers that Christ saves us by taking our nature upon him. If this had been all the Fathers had to say, we should conclude that we are saved by the Incarnation rather than by the Cross. This was far from their thought, but the two sides of their teaching were never quite harmonised. Their doctrine of the

Incarnation may be called strictly theological or philosophical in distinction from their doctrine of the Cross which by comparison was mythological or pictorial or poetic or mystical or symbolic. When they speak of the Cross, they tend to become lyrical. Thus, for instance, St. John of Damascus explains that the Christian religion, or at least that part of it which centres round the Cross of Christ, is unintelligible except to faith: that is, it presupposes religious experience, whether of the Church as a whole or of the individual. By the Cross, he says, "death is abolished, the sin of our first parent is liquidated, Hades is despoiled, the resurrection is bestowed, we are given power to despise the things of the present and death itself, the way is made straight for us to return to our pristine blessedness, the gates of Paradise are thrown open, human nature is given a seat at God's right hand, we are made children of God and heirs." Here, obviously, is no uniform and systematic doctrine of the Atonement; we have rather a confusion and cornucopia of metaphors and images as in the writings of the Apostle Paul. Later in the same chapter he says, "the Cross is a shield and weapon against the devil; it is the trophy set up by the Victor over him; it is the resurrection of them that are prostrate, the strong support of them that stand, the staff whereon the weak may lean, the shepherd's crook to the flock; it leads by the hand those who are eager; it is the perfection of those that are advanced; it is salvation of soul and body; there is not an evil but it turns aside; it is the cause of every good; it takes away sin; it is the plant of resurrection, the tree of life eternal."

This, we may say, is edifying rather than illuminating, but before we can come to a doctrine of our redemption, we must see clearly that which has to be explained. What must have been the life of the Church, what the inner experience of St. John himself, that he should so break out into poetry or rhapsody at the mention of the Cross! St. John wrote in the days when the Church in the East was meeting the onslaught of ruthless and triumphant Islam. The Christians, as we should gather from these passages, have been lifted above the fear of anything that life can bring and above the fear of death; they have a sense of sins forgiven, of having become the children of God, heirs of the eternal and heavenly world. The Cross is the symbol of Christ's victory.

I

The idea that the work of the Redeemer is to be interpreted in terms of Victory is recurrent throughout the history of the Church. Our Lord "was manifested that he might destroy the works of the devil"; he is, as he himself put it, the Stronger One who binds the strong man, Satan. It was near to the heart of Luther's religious apprehension that Christ has delivered us from death and sin, the devil and the law. It is thus put in the familiar English hymn:

> He breaks the power of cancelled sin,
> He sets the prisoner free.

The same *motif* runs through many of the great medieval hymns. Sin, Death, Satan are defeated by the crucified and risen Lord.

In the theology of the early Fathers this conception often took on grotesque forms—as it seems to us—a defeating of the enemy of souls by trickery. Thus, for instance, the demon called Death is represented as a great fish which swallows all mankind; there is Christ on the Cross; Death eagerly approaches, swallows the bait, which is the body of Christ, is caught on the hook of the divinity of Christ, and having tasted the spotless and life-giving body he is destroyed and restores all those whom previously he swallowed! The image strikes us as bizarre and even horrible. None the less, it is worth our while to look below the surface, for, apart from the strange image, something of the same sort is said by the Apostle Paul. He writes of the hidden wisdom of God "which none of the princes of this world knew, for, had they known it, they would not have crucified the Lord of glory." The "princes of this world" are not the representatives of the Roman empire but the fallen angels. It is to their evil machinations that St. Paul here ascribes the crucifixion. They thought and hoped that Christ being crucified was dead and done for; but they were deceived; it was impossible that he should be holden of death. This is all very far from our modern ways of speech, but perhaps is not so far

43

as we imagine from our modern ways of thought. For the mythology corresponds with human experience and intuition.

Thus, it is written in the book of Ecclesiasticus that the souls of the righteous are in the hands of God, and no torment can touch them; in the eyes of the foolish they seem to have died, but they are at peace; the foolish are deceived. When the news spread round Jerusalem on Good Friday that Christ was condemned and crucified and dead, we may conceive that a great sigh of relief ascended from his enemies. They were jubilant, but how bitterly they were deceived! They thought that their diplomacy had triumphed over him, that death had caught him and would hold him. Sin and Death had won the victory, it seemed; all the powers of darkness, of treachery, of pride, of fanaticism did him to death and thought they had triumphed over him. All the forces of evil were leagued against him in that one short hour; but he rose in glory, and from that moment the conquests of his Kingdom were visible for all to see. How easily and inevitably we also have here slipped into the language of mythology! By "powers of darkness" and "forces of evil" we do not mean fallen angels, nor, on the other hand, do we merely mean individual men. All the powers of darkness, all the terrors that beset man, all the despair that overwhelms him, all the mysterious forces of evil may well be summed up under the figure of Death. The last enemy, the enemy who in himself sums up all the forces that darken life and in the end destroy it, is Death. And Christ is

Death of death and hell's destruction.

Death caught him, but it could not hold him; he rose in victory.

So far we can imaginatively follow this language of victory, and even the queer simile of the body of Christ as the bait might be translated into modern terms. Thus, Christ was the supreme challenge to all the forces of darkness in the world; at all costs he must be destroyed; Herodians and Pharisees must forget their enmity; Pharisees and Sadducees must for once co-operate; Judah must work hand in hand for once with Rome —anything to be rid of him! Like a magnet he drew upon himself all the forces and reserves of evil; he compelled them to a supreme and final test; they must break him, or he will infallibly break them. And they thought they had succeeded when they crucified the Lord, but they were bitterly deceived, and he was Victor. If we substitute "magnet" for "bait," the image no longer seems grotesque, and we have some insight into what is meant.

Death was not only deceived, he was destroyed. Perishing himself he had to restore, to vomit forth, as it were, all those whom previously he had swallowed. The deliverance effected by the victory of Christ avails for all human nature. Hell-gate is broken down; the ancient prisoners are free; Christ has thrown open the gates of everlasting life to all believers. The terror of death, the power of death, the bondage of death are gone. What a pall of darkness lowered over mankind, over the living and the dead, and now it is as when the morning light scatters the shadows and the terrors of the night! No doubt we must attempt to express this faith in more modern or satisfactory terms; but before we can restate it, we must share it. Here is a proclamation of a victory that occurred in time, and yet is super-temporal. This is the Easter faith!

The immortality of the soul is a Greek doctrine; it is not Biblical. The Hebrews and the Christians spoke of resurrection. That is the language, not of survival, but of victory. The idea that the human soul is indestructible and therefore immortal may, or may not, be true, but there is little comfort in it. Thoughtless people often surmise that they will survive death and hope that, if they do, they will find existence somewhat less trying beyond the grave. But death means much more than the extinction of physical life; it is bondage to corruption, to sin, to self, to circumstance, to hopelessness; it has a spiritual as well as a physical aspect. We are apt to argue that Christ's resurrection, if we can believe it, assures us of our own survival. But that is to see in Christ's resurrection little more than the return of Lazarus from the grave. It is to fall far short of the triumphant conviction of the early Church that Christ had won the victory not merely over physical death but also over sin and despair and every kind of spiritual bondage.

45

II

The early theologians are haunted by a feeling or intuition for which they can find no scientific expression. God, they said, can indeed do anything; he could redeem man in any way he would, yet somehow it would not be quite fitting that God should redeem man by the mere word of his omnipotence; after all, we must "give the devil his due." Even the devil must be fairly treated; we have become his legitimate property; God will not expropriate him without recompense. There was, therefore, a special fitness in the manner of our deliverance; the tangled skein was unwound, it was not cut; there was a perfect "harmony" between the story of man's fall and the story of his redemption. By a woman he was tempted in the beginning; through a woman the Saviour came at last; by the fruit of one tree he fell, by the mystic fruit of another tree he was redeemed. Thus Christ "recapitulated" in his person the story of the human race. The devil, once victorious, was fairly and squarely defeated in open battle.

It is difficult to put this in satisfactory terms, but it points to a truth which comes back again and again to us when we consider sin and its forgiveness. It may, perhaps, be crudely illustrated in this way: a man is offered a great prize if he can win it in fair fight. He engages the enemy; later, when he is all but defeated and beaten to his knees, it is said to him, "You need not fight any more; you can have the prize." The man replies, "that is not fair; it can never be really mine unless I have won it in fair combat." Goodness, character, holiness have to be won, or they cannot be ours. In the nature of things we cannot be presented with character; we must achieve it. But in this life-battle against death and sin and circumstance and self we all fight a losing battle, and, if we are told that we ourselves must win the victory, we shall be cast into despair. Man must offer to God a perfect love, a perfect obedience. That of himself he cannot do—nor, it would seem, can God here help him, for that which is done with the help of another is not perfectly done by a man himself. A carpenter, for instance, who can only make a table with help is therein an

46

imperfect carpenter. The victory, therefore, must be won "in man, for man" over the foe; man himself must triumph over sin and offer a perfect love, a perfect obedience to God. This perfect love and perfect obedience, then, were offered by Christ, and he has called us brethren and identified himself with us for time and for eternity. Here we are back at the idea of the last chapter that we are one in Christ who has made himself one with us, and who by identifying himself with us has brought victory to all mankind, so that we receiving new life from him may be "changed from glory into glory," that "when he shall appear again in power and great glory we," being purified, "may be made like unto him." Many deep thoughts for meditation are here. At the moment we are concerned with one only, that death and the devil and sin must be honestly beaten, otherwise, to use schoolboy slang, our redemption "is not really fair." We are still far from being able to put this in satisfactory theological terms. But we can see, dimly at least, that it befits the glory of God, the divine "harmony," that our redemption should be a real victory, not a consolation prize.

III

Yet this talk of a victory over sin and death for all men, of "giving the devil his due," may well seem to many readers remote, mythological, unreal. It does not come down to earth. We may answer that, if in part Christ's victory over Satan is invisible and in the sphere of faith, in part it is visible and demonstrable. Consider, says St. John of Damascus, the actual victory of Christ, "the achievements of his Presence, the marks of his Power." See, the worship of the demons has come to an end; altars and temples of the idols have been swept away; the knowledge of God has been implanted; there has been an ethical revival; new hope has come to mankind; a new era has dawned such that we can say, that the creation has been sanctified by the blood of Christ. All this, he says, has been achieved by the Cross and Passion of our Lord; the Good News has been broadcast throughout the world by the medium, not of victorious armies, but of those who were "naked, poor, unlettered, persecuted, tormented, done to death"; it is these who have prevailed over the wise and the powerful by the preaching of the Cross; for these poor preachers were accompanied by "the invincible power of the Crucified." Death, in the past man's greatest terror, has been defeated; and all this victory has been achieved by "gentleness and long-suffering and persuasion."

It is very difficult for us to avoid "mythological" language, whether we be men of religion or not. Our scientists, if they are not Christians, often speak of that which is achieved by "Nature" or by "Evolution" or by "Natural Selection." Sir Charles Sherrington, for instance, uses these figures of speech in his recent Gifford Lectures; he tells us, too, that electrons, protons and neurons are mental figments, that energy is a space-time figment, and that things are "electric charges." Yet no one doubts that the scientists, however inexact or mythological or unsatisfactory their language, are telling us about the real and actual world. To speak of "demonic forces" is no more mythological, and is probably much more exact, than to speak of "economic forces," for there is no philosophical reason why there should not be disembodied evil intelligences, whereas an "economic force" is a mere abstraction. When, then, we say that Christ won the victory over Sin and Death, we speak of a victory that is partly invisible and acknowledged by faith alone, but like the scientists we are speaking also about that which shows its effects in the real and actual world. St. John could point in his day to the palpable triumph of the Church over the Roman Empire that had sought to extirpate the Name of Christ. We likewise can point to the triumphs of the Cross in our own time. The last century and a half has seen an undermining of the citadel of faith from many quarters—from "science," from psychology, from the break-up of the old Biblical dogmatism and of the traditional theologies, from the comparative study of religion; indeed, there was probably never a time when the faith was assailed from so many sides at once. Yet it is in these years that the Christian Church has spread and triumphed, in Asia and in Africa, as never since the first centuries. In these very days, the Church is suffering a persecution more protracted and more ruthless and more widespread than ever it has known before, yet it grows stronger in every land. Let no man say, then, that the victory of Christ is mere mythology or phantasy!

When St. John of Damascus has enumerated the triumphs of the Cross in the soul and in the world, he breaks out in an apostrophe to Christ: "hail, O Christ, Word of God and Wisdom and Power and God Almighty!" What, he asks, can we render to him in return? We can render nothing; we can only receive —our salvation; and such is his goodness that he is grateful to us for being his beneficiaries. This is the "inexpressible condescension" of Almighty God.

IV

After describing what we may call the external effects of the Cross such as the despoiling of Hades and the opening of the gates of Paradise, St. John turns to the internal or individual effects. The Cross, he reminds his readers, was marked as a sign upon the believer's forehead in baptism; it corresponds, therefore, with circumcision which is the distinguishing mark of Jews. The Cross is a "shield" and "weapon" and "trophy" against the devil; it is a "seal" like the blood upon the doorposts at the Passover; it is "the perfection of the proficient," a "tree of eternal life."

This is the lyrical language of devotion. What precisely is meant by the shield and weapon and trophy? Is it the historic Cross on Calvary, or is it the cross signed on the forehead of the believer, or is it the Word of the Cross, the Gospel itself? It might reasonably be argued that in this passage the "tree of eternal life" must be the historic Cross, that it is the Cross signed on the believer's forehead which corresponds to the blood on the lintel of the doors at the first Passover, and that the "perfection of the proficient" is the Word of the Cross, the Gospel. But these distinctions which we make might not have appeared significant or legitimate to St. John. He would say, I think, that there is, and can be, but one Cross of our redemption, though it may exist in many modes. A modern illustration of this principle will make it clear. When a house is built, there is first the house in the mind of the architect, second there is the house on the blueprint, third there is the house in bricks and mortar. St. John, if I understand him aright, would say that the house in the architect's mind, the house on the blue-print and the house in bricks and mortar are the same house in three different modes of being. Thus the architect, when he sees the building, says "that is my house," meaning, "that is the house which once existed only in my mind, which later I drew, and which now exists also in bricks and mortar." Technical philosophers have much to say about the propriety of speaking of the house as existing in three modes, but it is easy to see that the expression corresponds with something real; this is all that matters for our present purpose. Thus St. John would have repudiated our distinctions by saying that the Cross on Calvary, the Cross on the believer's forehead and the Cross preached, are three modes of existence of one eternal Cross. The historic event on Calvary, its meaning, its representation in preaching, its "showing forth" in sacraments are all modes of one divine action, one event, which we term the Cross.

In the course of Christian history some have laid all the stress upon the historic Cross as achieving our redemption by some august transaction accomplished once for all; others have laid all stress upon the preaching of the Cross, and therefore upon our redemption as answering to the response of faith; others, again, have interpreted the work of our redemption chiefly in terms of the sacraments as means of grace. The Greek Fathers suggest to us that each of these views is partial by itself. There is the one divine action of God's self-giving for our redemption; this was realised in history when Christ was "crucified under Pontius Pilate"; this same divine action is brought home to us in the preaching of the Word; similarly the sacraments are not a mere symbol of Calvary nor a repetition of Calvary; but that very same thing which Calvary was is brought to us in the bread and wine. The Cross is God's Word to man. The preaching of the Cross is that same Word of God to man; the sacrament conveys the same divine Word in another mode. This is indicated by the words of institution which have come down to us—"do this in memory of me." To the English reader this suggests that the celebration of the Holy Supper is a mere memorial rite, but the word "memory" in the Aramaic has a different feel. When the widow woman, seeing her dead child, said to the prophet Elijah, "art thou come to call my sin to remembrance?", she did not mean, "art thou come to bring back to memory things I had long buried in the past"; she meant, rather, "hast thou brought my sin up into the present out of the past, so that it is once more to-day an actual, potent thing, and because of it my son is dead?" The "remembrance" of Christ at the Communion is not a recollection of an event long past, it is a bringing of that past right down into the present, so that it is present and operative now. The Communion or the faithful and powerful preaching of the Cross is not the reminder of Calvary, but the bringing of Calvary itself down into the present, to the souls and bodies of the worshippers.

Our redemption, then, may be regarded in terms of the Victory of Christ. It is a cosmic victory; that is to say, though it took place at a certain hour in the world's history and a definite point on the world's surface, it affects the past and the future, the visible world and the invisible. Yet is this no mythological victory, a phantasy of human self-deception. Its effects can be clearly seen within the course of history, as witness the conversion of the Roman Empire in the fourth century or the marvellous spread of the faith in the nineteenth and twentieth centuries. Moreover, it is a victory that is realized in the hearts and lives of believers. The Cross of Christ is no mere distant event in history, it is an active and redeeming constituent of the present. Not the memory of it but the Cross itself—the redeeming, victorious act of God in Christ—is brought home to us through the ministries of the Church in preaching and in sacrament.

CHAPTER VI

The Way, the Truth and the Life

This chapter takes its quotations chiefly from St. Augustine of Hippo in North Africa, the author of *The Confessions* and many other works. He lived from A.D. 354–430. He saw the beginnings of the break-up of the Roman Empire of the West. He more than the Fathers of the East takes us back to "the Jesus of history" and interprets our salvation as a coming home to God through Jesus Christ who is to us the Way, the Truth and the Life. Christ weans us from the love of the world to the love of God which is the true end of man. St. Augustine interprets our union with Christ in personal and ethical terms.

Mr. Burnaby's *Amor Dei* (Hodder & Stoughton) is important but not very easy reading. The *Confessions of St. Augustine*, available in many editions, should be studied. His *City of God* is published in the Temple Classics in translation.

Questions for discussion: (1) In what sense is Christ our example? What does copying him involve? (2) How far is sin a matter of ignorance? (3) Is it through the humanity of Christ that we come to faith in his divinity? (4) What is the part of the Holy Spirit in our Redemption? (5) What is the motive of the Christian life? (6) What does St. Augustine mean when he says that "we have been made Christ"?

IN the last two chapters we have looked primarily to the Eastern Church for light upon the subject of our redemption. When we turn to the West, we find, of course, the same Gospel, the same faith, and not infrequently the same theological terms; yet we breathe a different air. The West asks different questions and sees different aspects of "the manifold wisdom of God."

St. Augustine is the father of medieval theology in the West. He is also the father of Protestant theology, both in its Lutheran and Calvinist forms. He was a prolific author who poured into sermons, letters, treatises and, occasionally, somewhat inferior verses the rich and varied harvest of his teeming mind. All schools of theology turn to St. Augustine, quote him and seek his authority. This is due not to his ambiguity but to the copiousness of his mind and thought. His hints, suggestions, insights cannot be reduced to a single tidy theological theory. We can hardly say of him that he had "a theology of our redemption." Our present purpose will be served if we can pick from his writings one or two ideas which may seem to have special significance for our thought to-day.

He was by nature and interest a psychologist; moreover, as he shows us in his *Confessions*, he had passed through a profound spiritual crisis in his conversion. We find accordingly that he gives an inward, ethical, personal interpretation to the doctrine of our redemption. He speaks of the work of Christ in terms of sacrifice; he has much to say of the "harmony" or fitness of our redemption by the defeat of Satan on the very field where he had been victorious; he sets forth Christ as the Conqueror; he has no dispute with the Greek Fathers, but more than they he is oppressed with the problem of human sin and expresses our redemption in terms of the sanctifying work of the holy Spirit.

I

Our Lord came not only as "a sacrifice for sin" but also as "an ensample of godly life." He delivers us from temptation not only by his assistance but also, says St. Augustine, by his example; God was made man that he might give us an example of humility; Christ is the heavenly Wisdom who came to show us the way to God. When we think of our redemption in terms of Christ's taking our nature upon him or in terms of his mysterious victory over all the powers of darkness, these vast conceptions seem somewhat remote; we are pointed to a heavenly transaction which we can but partially and dimly understand. St. Augustine turns our thoughts to "the Jesus of history," to the Gospel narratives, to "the Man Christ Jesus." It is through his humanity, he says, that we know his divinity; he in his incarnate life shows us the way to God; learning from the Gospels we discover that he is himself the way to God. Thus St. Augustine in simple and human language sets forth our redemption in terms of our finding our way back to God through the teaching, as well as the Passion, of the Son of

God. Christ, he says in one of his sermons, "because he is the Truth and the Life with the Father, is the Word of God of whom it is said, 'The life was the light of men.' Since, then, he is the Truth and the Life with the Father, and we had no way to come to the truth, the Son of God, who ever is the Truth and the Life in the Father, by assuming humanity was made the Way. Walk by the Man, and thou comest to God. Through him thou travellest, to him thou travellest. Look not for any way by which thou mayest come to him except himself. For had he been unwilling to be our way, we must for ever have wandered. He therefore was made the Way by which thou art to come. I say not to thee, Go looking for the way. The Way itself has come to thee; arise and walk. Walk I mean not physically but morally."

Christ is the Way to God; it is he who leads us to God. He not only brings us into the way but he accompanies us upon it. "Lead me, O Lord, in thy way, and I shall walk in thy truth." St. Augustine thus comments on this verse from the psalms: "Thy way, thy truth, thy life is Christ. . . . 'I am the way and the truth and the life. Lead me, O Lord, in thy way.' . . . How does he lead? Always by admonition, always by giving thee his hand. . . . For by giving thee his Christ, he gives his hand; by giving his hand, he gives his Christ. He brings into the way by conducting to his Christ; he leads in the way by leading in his Christ. For Christ is the Truth. 'Lead me therefore, O Lord, in thy way, and I shall walk in thy truth'; that is, in him who says, 'I am the way and the life and the truth.' For thou who leadest in the way and the truth, whither dost thou conduct except to life? Thou leadest therefore in him and to him. 'Lead me, O Lord, in thy way, and I shall walk in thy truth'."

Here is a profound truth about our redemption, very different from the aspects we have hitherto considered. It is so simple that a child can understand it. Redemption is deliverance from error, from false judgments, from failure to see the meaning of life; it is the homeward journey of the soul to God. Our Lord is the Good Shepherd who goes out after the lost sheep, brings it into the right way, and leads it home. When we speak of souls as "lost," we should mean not that they are condemned to eternal punishment (for that we cannot assert), but that they are wandering and lost and cannot find the way home. That is the state of all men apart from Christ. Their affliction is not that they are necessarily wicked (for they may be of far nobler character than many Christians) but that they are literally lost. Christ brings the truth—the truth about God, the truth about ourselves, the truth about life. Walking in the light of that truth, we are on our way home to God; so to walk is to live, for any other kind of life is a kind of death. We are redeemed by our Lord as he is the Way, the Truth and the Life.

Our redemption means that we must come home to God. What is the way? Here Christ is our example and our Guide. Our redemption is deliverance from error and darkness, from misunderstanding God and misunderstanding life. Christ not only gives us the truth, he is the Truth; he is not merely a Teacher whose words are recorded for us from the past, he is also the living Truth who speaks directly to our hearts. Our redemption is from death to life. This means much more than that, when we are dead, we shall be raised from the dead into the heavenly world. It means that we are delivered now into "life that is life indeed" from a state of living which is a living death. Christ is our Life.

This way of putting things is almost an affront to many orthodox persons; they are offended that so many of their familiar catchwords are missing from it. They say, "that will never do; there is nothing about the Cross in that way of putting things; you are offering a merely human Jesus; this is just 'Humanitarianism,' 'Liberalism,' 'Modernism'." Now, all religious statements have, if we may so put it, a shallow meaning and a deep meaning. A man might say that Christ is to him the Way and the Truth and the Life meaning thereby that he presumed to take Christ for his "guide, philosopher and friend." He would be a Christian much as another man might be a Platonist or a Marxist. But at the deeper level at which these words are meant, they hold in them all the mystery of the Incarnation. And, says Professor Karl Adam, "this is the way of the faith, *per Jesum ad Christum*," it is through the human that the divine is known to us.

There is a further important apologetic advantage in this way of approaching our question. Our redemption is indeed a mystery of grace, but we have often made it unnecessarily mysterious to beginners by presenting it in philosophical and theological or even mythological terms. We should perhaps be wiser and, incidentally, closer to the first apologists for the Christian faith, if we speak first of our redemption in terms of our Lord as Way and Life and Truth, for there is something here that appeals directly to the reason and the conscience of all men except those whose hearts are hardened.

Then, further, Christ has united humanity to himself in his Incarnation; he has won the victory over the powers of darkness, but it is well we be reminded that Christ can do nothing *for* us if he do not also something *in* us. Our redemption is completed beyond the grave, but it must be begun in our hearts now. It has been customary amongst theologians to divide theories of the Atonement into three main classes, the transactional, the representational and the Moral Influence Theory. This last, though sponsored by the late Dean Rashdall and Dr. R. S. Franks, has been repudiated by most orthodox theologians and can, no doubt, by shallow minds be represented as if no more was to be seen in our redemption than the influence of Christ's life and teaching upon our consciousness. The little word "only" has been the bane of theology. Christ has not done "only" this, but this he has done, and it is a vital element in our redemption. The Gospel is simple, and it can be understood by simple people. It is not necessary to be a philosopher or a theologian to be redeemed or even to understand, as a man may, what redemption is. "Through Christ thou comest to Christ," says St. Augustine: "How through Christ to Christ? Through Christ the Man to Christ the God: through the Word made flesh to the Word that in the beginning was God with God: from that which man ate to that which daily the angels eat." In another sermon he says, "Through Christ the Man thou proceedest to Christ the God. Far from thee is God, but God was made man. That which was far removed from thee has been brought near through him who was made man. The place of thine abiding is God; the road thou travellest is man. The road by which thou travellest and the goal to which thou travellest are the same Christ himself."

It is in this way that St. Augustine more than other theologians relates the work of Christ to the work of the holy Spirit. Our redemption is the work of Christ in us as well as the work of Christ on our behalf.

II

For what is man made? What is the meaning of life? To these ultimate questions the Christian answer is quite clear. We were made that we might love God and cleave to him for ever. It is important to dwell upon this because, though it is obvious, it is not obvious to all. Many to-day, if asked what they conceive to be life's meaning, would answer that life is a mystery, and they do not pretend to see its meaning, but they feel bound to live honourable, decent, useful lives, so far as they can, and they hope that somehow this will prove to have been the right thing in the end. In fact, they deliberately set ultimate questions aside and get on with the business of life. Others would answer that the purpose of life is that we learn to be good and ultimately go to our reward in heaven. Others, again, would say that the purpose of life is service. These are not ignoble answers, and they are not wholly false; but they are not ultimate answers. The ultimate answer is that God made us for himself, that we should love him with all our heart and mind and soul and strength, and love all men for his sake. We, who are caught in the meshes of sin, are far from a love of that kind; if we could so love, we should be redeemed.

Thus, says St. Augustine, the purpose of Christ's coming was to awaken love in us. First of all it was necessary to persuade us how great is the love of God for us; "therefore he must persuade man how much God has loved us and of what nature are those whom he has loved, the former lest we despair, the latter lest we be exalted." There has been force in the objection made by outsiders that the Christian's preoccupation with his own salvation has been a selfish interest. If we do right and even endure hardship in order that we may get to heaven, we may merely be acting from motives of prudence without any religion whatsoever. But, if we love God, then we not only rejoice that he is what he is, but we find calling and guidance everywhere, and we do all things for the love of him. Then, indeed, we are redeemed from self and from the world for God.

St. Augustine says that in this world it is quite impossible for us to be truly happy or blessed; yet the trouble with most people is that they are too happy after a fashion and love the world too much. There are many beautiful things in the world, and God made them; it is right, therefore, that we should rejoice in them, but if we enjoy them without remembering whose gift they are and what love lies behind them, we make God's own gifts an occasion of being unfaithful to him. It is as if, says St. Augustine, a bridegroom made his bride a ring, and she cared for the ring she received more than for the bridegroom who made it for her; surely her heart would be shown unfaithful in the very gift of her bridegroom! We are like that. We enjoy such happiness as life offers—and complain bitterly when things go wrong with us and all is not to our taste; but not receiving these good gifts as the gifts of God with thankfulness, we are alienated from life's real purpose and ultimately find all life meaningless.

To love God and to praise him in the happiness of life—that is part of our redemption; but to praise him and rejoice in him in our pains and sorrows is to see yet deeper into the heavenly mystery. This is illustrated by Lukeria in Turgenev's story *The Living Relic*. The story is thus epitomised by Mrs. Gorodetzky:

> Lukeria, the village beauty and its best singer, fell by accident from a staircase. Withered, paralysed, left alone in a remote hut, hardly ever visited by anyone, she is all love and praise of God. She does not pray much: "Why should I worry the Lord God? What can I ask of him? He knows better than I do what I need. He had sent me a cross which signifies that he loves me. We are commanded to understand it so." This last remark is not that of protest but of whole-hearted acceptance.

Such an attitude to pain, suffering and disaster is so alien to our natural and conventional ways of thought that it seems to us at first sight almost morbid. But in fact it is typically Christian, it is the decisive victory over the world, it is precisely our redemption from the world.

This, for instance, is from the servant-girl, quoted in Chapter I from *They Found God* by Miss M. L. Christlieb:

> When I consider the great advantages of being a servant, I cannot cease to praise God for making me one. No other state in the world would be so dear to me. I can live in it quietly without any taking note of me. Who would think of paying respect to a poor servant? Anyone may rebuke her, look down on her, find fault with what she does or says. Is not that the most excellent school of humility? In what other state could one learn so well? For this reason should not all servants consider themselves fortunate? When servants complain to me of the very things that should help them, I am astonished; I say in my mind, if only you knew how salutary it is to be blamed and despised and kept strictly you would rejoice instead of grieving! But how few know the blessedness of suffering with Christ in being rejected of men and having to bear their contempt. To me it became a pleasure when I saw others preferred before me, when the least in the house held me to be lower than they. I learned, too, to take pleasure in taking the wishes and likings of others before my own. My old nature felt this to be difficult, but my spirit rejoiced in it. I liked submitting to the lowest as if they had been high saints, for I did not look at the person I obeyed but at Him for whose sake I obeyed. I did not serve men as men; I worked as if serving God himself in his Presence. . . . I do not know what it means to have an enemy—I never had one. Those one might call enemies I consider my greatest friends. I only distinguish them from others because I love them more. When anyone is rude to me, he is immediately received into my heart and has a share in my prayers, though I never thought of him before. In all ways possible to me I strive to win souls for my love. I would willingly suffer being cast into hell, if by that I might prevent any soul for whom my Love died losing her way. I weep for their sins; I call to God day and night for forgiveness for them. When I perceive their spiritual dangers, great anxiety and fear comes over me. Give me a voice to reach all the world, I prayed, to call to them to leave sin and love thee! If only I could give my heart to them, or collect everyone's in mine! Then I should throw them all into the fire of thy love. How can I live and see thy love misunderstood or despised?"

Contrast with this the proud Stoic ideal which steels the hear against suffering and the misadventures of this passing life Part of the meaning of redemption is that we accept as of God's appointment and as from a Father's hand whatsoever life may bring to us, that we do all things for the love of God, and in all things rejoice in him. We are called to imitate Christ, says St. Augustine, not in respect of the wonders that he did but as he was meek and lowly in heart. Redemption is, indeed, the life of Christ in us.

III

In the typical teaching of the Eastern Church, as we saw, our redemption is wrought by the Incarnation of the Son of God whereby human nature is taken up into the divine nature. St. Augustine also uses such bold language. "By loving God we are made divine," he says; "wonder and rejoice," he writes elsewhere, "we have been made Christ; for, if he is the head and we are the members, the whole man is he and we. . . . Till we all come to the unity of faith and the knowledge of the Son of God, to the perfect man, to the measure of the stature of the fulness of Christ.' The fulness of Christ, then, is the Head and members. What is Head and members? Christ and the Church. We should indeed be guilty of pride in arrogating such a position to ourselves had not the promise been vouchsafed to us by him who through his apostles says, 'Now ye are the Body of Christ and members.' The apostle says likewise, 'as in the body we have many members, but, though all the members of the body are many, yet is the body one; so also is Christ.'" He means, explains St. Augustine, that Head and body constitute one Christ. But all this, as is made abundantly plain, is not to be understood as if divinity were somehow injected into humanity like a drug into the body; it is to be understood ethically and spiritually. We are united to God as sin is beaten down in us: "we may only deem our sins conquered when they are conquered by the love of God; this love is the gift of God himself alone, and it comes to us solely through the Mediator between God and man, the Man Christ Jesus, who was caused to participate in our mortality that he might make us partakers of his divinity."

So far, then, St. Augustine has suggested to us that our redemption is wrought for us by Christ as he awakens our hearts, offers us an example, becomes for us the Way, the Truth and the Life, and evokes in us the love of God, whereby we both triumph over life and are united with Christ himself.

CHAPTER VII

Sin

Redemption is from sin. We have "free will," but this does not
mean that we can always will what is good. There is that which the
theologians call "original sin": there is a corruption in our nature.
Since we cannot heal ourselves, our Redemption is by the grace and
initiative of God. Sin is "inordinate love," that is, it is the pursuit of
lower ends to the despite of God and our own true good, which is to
love God and cleave to him for ever. Sin is also pride; our pride must
be broken that we may enter the Kingdom of God. It is the Cross
that breaks and heals us.

For this chapter also St. Augustine's *Confessions* should be consulted.
See also St. Thomas à Kempis on *The Imitation of Christ*. *The Doctrine
of Sin in Relation to Modern Thought* is discussed by the Bishop of
Gloucester in the *Church Quarterly Review*, No. CCLVII for October–
December, 1939. Better than theological reading about sin would be
a study of the Passion narrative in the Gospels with the question, what
sins are here revealed in man, and are they not our own sins?

Questions that arise: (1) Can we always will to do the right? (2) Does
the doctrine of "original sin" correspond with the data of history and
of our own experience? (3) How can our wills be renewed? (4) Is St.
Augustine's rule, "Love, and then do as you please," sufficient?
(5) How does the Cross reveal sin? (6) How does the Cross break
our pride?

REDEMPTION is, first and last, from sin. It is sometimes said
that the Eastern Fathers were concerned with redemption
from corruption rather than from sin. That, I think, is a misunderstanding; but it is true that the Eastern Fathers laid the
greatest stress upon the freedom of the will, while the Western
Fathers, led by St. Augustine, were feelingly aware of the
bondage of the will. The problem of "free will" is the source
of interminable discussions which reach no conclusion, but
when St. Augustine speaks of the bondage of the will, he is
pointing to a truth that we all can recognise. He is not denying
the obvious fact that man can choose. Even animals have "free

will" in a sense. If a dog puts up a rabbit, no outside force compels it to give chase; we may say, if we will, that the dog acts voluntarily. Yet obviously the dog which is off like a streak is not really and effectively free to continue its careless progress; every instinct drives it to the chase. Similarly, it is true enough that no one compels the habitual drunkard to enter the public house; he goes there voluntarily; yet it would be at least as true to say that he goes "against his will," he cannot help himself. "That which I would not I do," said the Apostle, therein expressing every man's experience. We are bidden love the Lord our God with all our heart and mind and soul and strength and our neighbour as ourselves. We can desire to do that, but can we will to do it?

I

We think of sins as actions which we know we ought not to have done. But St. Augustine's analysis goes much deeper. We need not merely the forgiveness of particular acts of sin; we need also redemption from moral blindness and moral impotence. The whole human race, he says, is subject to sin, and "herein is the most just penalty of sin that a man loses the faculty to do good when he has been unwilling to exercise it, though otherwise, had he willed it, right action would have been easy. He who against his better knowledge does not act rightly loses the knowledge of what is right; and he who has refused to do right, when he could, loses the power to do right when he will. For in truth there is for every sinning soul a double penalty, loss of knowledge and loss of power." St. Augustine realized the radical nature of our malady. His point is put in modern terms by the Archbishop of Canterbury thus:

> The centre of the trouble is not the turbulent appetites, though they are troublesome enough, and the human faculty for imagination increases their turbulence. But the centre of trouble is the personality as a whole, which is self-centred and can only be wholesome and healthy if it is God-centred. The whole personality in action is the will; and it is the will which is perverted. Our primary need is not to control our passions by our purpose, but to direct our purpose itself to the right end. It is the form taken by our knowledge

of good and evil that perverts our nature. We know good
and evil, but we know them amiss. We take them into our lives
but we mis-take them. The corruption is at the centre of rational
and purposive life.

Sin, then, is not just a series of wrong acts which we, being
free and rational beings, could quite well have avoided had we
exercised our wills; it is a bondage from which of ourselves
we cannot escape; it is an inner perversion of reason and will,
a disease of the soul from which no man can deliver himself.
Nor can we wholly blame ourselves personally for this impotence and blindness. In part at least it is our evil inheritance
"in Adam," that is, as members of the "fallen" human race.
Prior to the actual, deliberate sins that we commit there is
"original sin."

This doctrine of "original sin" has received short shrift at
the hands of many moderns. It is monstrous, they say, to speak
of little new-born children as guilty of sin; they are, on the
contrary, the type of innocence, and our Lord said of them
that "of such is the Kingdom of Heaven"; the doctrine, therefore, that little children need to be cleansed, or can be cleansed,
from sin in baptism has no basis in Scripture and is morally
repellent. There is force in this; little children are not guilty
creatures; it is we who must be converted and become like them
if we would enter the Kingdom; it is blasphemy to suggest
that God will condemn such as die in infancy to eternal damna-
tion because through no fault of their own they have never
been baptized. Moreover, we cannot think of sin as something
which is physically transmitted from generation to generation.

None the less, this doctrine of "original sin" corresponds
with a spiritual fact which we cannot well escape. We may
put it in this way: sin is a self-determination; that is, the sins I
commit to-day are the result of the kind of person I am, and
the kind of person I am now depends upon the kind of person
I was yesterday, and so on back through all the years. Sin or
wrong choice is the result of earlier sin and of wrong choices.
But then, logically, there must have been some first sin at the
beginning. But how did I come to commit my first sin? That
at least I cannot ascribe to previous sins, for it is the first; nor

can I say that it was a deliberate conscious first choice of evil, for it goes back before memory to earliest childhood. Since, then, sin is a self-determination, and my first sin cannot be ascribed to previous sins, the conclusion is inevitable that there is some taint or flaw in the human nature we inherit; for, although about any particular sin we can always say that "we need not have done it," we know very well that being human we could not have been sinless. Our will is somehow weak or perverted from the first.

Again, what we choose depends very largely upon what we think, that is, upon our judgment of what is good and worth while and to be aimed at. But from our earliest infancy, however happy and good our homes, we grow up in a society where wrong judgments about God, about people, about life are "in the air"; we breathe in wrong ideas from the beginning, and we could not always will the right because we often cannot see the right. As human beings growing up in this world we are inevitably caught up in this vast network of worldly judgments and unworthy ideas about God; the bondage of sin must hold us all.

Furthermore, every child, naturally and not sinfully, is the centre of its own little universe; only very slowly does it learn unselfishness. Our personality, as the Archbishop puts it, is self-centred, and it must become God-centred, for only so is our human nature what it is meant to be. "Behold, I was shapen in iniquity, and in sin did my mother conceive me!"

Thus our redemption from sin is not merely the forgiveness of past sins but our deliverance from this whole world of perversion and sin and self-reference which is our inheritance "in Adam." We can no more save ourselves than we can lift ourselves "by our own waist-band." The initiative, therefore, if we are to be saved, must come from God.

There are those who prefer to keep the term "sin" for deliberate acts of which we are personally guilty, and to speak of "moral disease" rather than "original sin"; but "original sin" by whatever name we call it is a palpable and tragic and universal fact, and it is intimately connected with the sacrament of baptism. Since, then, baptism is thus associated with redemption, something must be said here about it. We cannot believe that God's final acceptance or rejection of a child's soul can depend upon a rite which a man has performed or has not performed; we do not think of baptism as being like the injection of a serum into the body; we interpret the rite spiritually, not superstitiously. It has many aspects; upon one only can we here insist. In a "Christian" country such as our own the distinction between the Church and the world is often hard to discern, for in some measure the world has been Christianized. In a non-Christian country such as India or Africa or even Nazi Germany the distinction between the Church and the world is obvious, even, often enough, to the outward eye. Baptism is a sacrament of the Church and cannot rightly be considered apart from the Church; it is the rite of admission into the Church. It must not be sundered in thought from the faith of the parents, the faith and fellowship of the Church, and its fulfilment in the rite of Confirmation. The Church is the fellowship of the redeemed, the sphere of the working of the Holy Spirit; in spite of all its glaring imperfections and sins it is the new humanity where the rule of God is accepted, the glory of God sought, and where by the renewing of our minds worldly judgments are put away and "the mind of Christ" is known; Christ is the life of the Church which, though it is in and of the world, is yet a supernatural society. Into this society the child of Christian parents is received by baptism which not only declares that long ago Christ died for this child, as indeed he died for all, but also most solemnly conveys to the child its right in the new humanity, the company of the redeemed, and seals in its case the promises of Christ which are to believing parents "and to their seed after them." If we think of "original sin" as the whole nexus of worldly judgments and the power of an un-Christian environment, then the Church is the sphere where "original sin" is put away in that Body of which Christ is the Head. As we can so easily see in a heathen country, the children of the Church live in a different atmosphere, a different world, from those without. Baptism is as solemn an act as the crowning of a king or the enthronement of an Archbishop; it is the conveyance and the seal of that redemption which Christ has wrought

66

for us, is working in us, and shall perfect in his consummated Kingdom.

We are thus redeemed by the renewing of our wills and the renewing of our minds; this is a process which takes place in the life and fellowship of the Church, and the Church arises directly from the Passion and Ascension of our Lord.

The initiative in our redemption is with God; not a step of the way can we go without the grace of God; yet, as we have seen, redemption is the way back to God; it is the way we ourselves must go; we must walk painfully that homeward road; sin must be vanquished in us as well as for us. St. Paul spoke of "the crown which the Lord, the righteous Judge, shall give me in that day"; there is a sense in which salvation must be "merited." That is a very dangerous word, for salvation is only of God, and the Christian must always say:

> Nothing in my hand I bring,
> Simply to thy Cross I cling.

None the less, our Lord speaks of "reward," even while everything is of the grace of God. Our salvation is the free gift of God, yet we have to "work out our salvation." St. Augustine deals with this difficulty when he treats of the text, "It is not of him that willeth nor of him that runneth but of God that sheweth mercy." He interprets this to mean that "the whole work belongs to God, who both makes the will of man righteous and thus prepares it for assistance, and assists it when prepared. For the man's righteousness of will precedes many of God's gifts, but not all; and it must itself be included among those which it does not precede. We read in Holy Scripture both that God's mercy shall 'go before me' and that his mercy shall 'follow me.' It goes before the unwilling to make him willing; it follows the willing to make his will effectual. Why are we taught to pray for our enemies, who are plainly unwilling to lead a holy life, unless that God may work willingness in them? And why are we ourselves taught to ask that we may receive, unless that he who has created in us the wish may himself satisfy the wish? We pray, then, for our enemies that the mercy of God may go before them; we pray for ourselves that his mercy

67

may follow us." God renews our wills that we may be able to will aright, and then by his grace he helps us. Thus, while all is of God, it is not apart from the co-operation of our wills.

II

Redemption is from sin. What exactly is sin? It has been interpreted and explained in many metaphors. In the Old Testament it is constantly represented as infidelity, the unfaithfulness of Israel to the Lord, "although I was an husband unto them." It is commonly spoken of as rebellion, and such it is against the law of God. But in St. Augustine two conceptions are most prominent, sin is the result of concupiscence and of pride.

(1) St. Augustine is pre-eminently the theologian of love. "It is by loving God that we are made divine." God is the *Summum Bonum*, the supreme good for man; man's true life and blessedness, therefore, consist in loving God. Thus sin, as Mr. Burnaby puts it, is negatively "the failure to love God; positively, it is the inevitable transference of love to objects which, though good because God's creatures, are goods less than the highest." We are bidden in Scripture, "whatsoever ye do, do all to the glory of God"; to act from any other motive is sinful. Sin, then, is not just one of a series of wicked actions such as theft or murder or fornication; it is that perversion of our personality which leads us to act from selfish motives, for our own pleasure and indulgence instead of for the love of God. Man always aims at the good; that is, every desire is for something which rightly or wrongly we conceive to be desirable, and, since this is God's world, his workmanship, all that he has made is in itself good and desirable. Sin is the *inordinate* desire of things which in themselves are good. For instance, leisure is good, and we should enjoy our leisure with thankful hearts before God; but to choose leisure when we ought to be at work is to desire that which is intrinsically good but at the moment wrong; this is sin. When our hearts are turned to God, we do not necessarily or probably abandon all the tasks that once we did; rather we do the old tasks in a new way with a new spirit and a new motive; instead of acting

primarily to earn a living or to avoid trouble or to win honour and reputation, we now act "that we may be well pleasing to him." It is as when a man falls in love and begins to live for his bride whereas before he had lived only for himself. All is sin that is not for the love of God.

The Christian life has too often been set out in a series of negatives; Christians have been told that they must avoid theatres or dance-halls or public-houses, as if God had not implanted in us the love of acting, as if dancing were intrinsically wicked, as if the devil, not God, were responsible for fermentation. There are, and there must be, prohibitions, "thou shalt not steal, thou shalt do no murder, thou shalt not covet," but these are, as it were, extreme cases. St Augustine lays down but one rule: "love, and then do as you please." "Seek ye first the Kingdom. . . . Thou shalt love the Lord thy God with all thy heart." St. Augustine sees all human history as the tension and opposition of two realms: "Thus two loves made the two realms; that is, the love of self to the contempt of God made the earthly realm, and the love of God to the contempt of self made the heavenly realm. The one glories in itself, the other in the Lord. The one lifts up its head in its own glory, the other says to its God, 'Thou art my glory, thou exaltest mine head.' In the one case the lust of power dominates in its chiefs or in those nations which it subjugates; in the other there is mutual service in charity from the leaders in seeking the common good, from the subjects in obedience. The one loves its own virtue in the persons of those who are powerful therein, the other says to its God, 'I will love thee, O Lord, who art my virtue.'" In other words, redemption is intimately connected with conversion, and conversion is that fundamental change whereby a man's centre of interest ceases to be himself, his ambitions, his desires, his demands upon life, and, instead, he accepts his life at the hands of God, seeks in all things the glory of God, and performs all his actions for the love of God. We are converted or redeemed in so far as we act from the motive of the love of God.

The process of our redemption is not yet complete. Self and selfish motives enter into, and mar, our most disinterested actions; so it is that Bishop Lancelot Andrewes could say without exaggeration, "all my life bewrayeth me." Christ came and taught and wrought and died that he might kindle in our hearts the love of God, and thus we might be redeemed. It is pre-eminently the sight of Christ upon the Cross that has awakened the love of God in the hearts of men:

> His dying crimson like a robe
> Spreads o'er his body on the Tree.
> Then am I dead to all the globe,
> And all the globe is dead to me.

(2) Sin is not only concupiscence or inordinate desire; it is also pride or "Titanism." It was the temptation in the beginning, "ye shall be as gods"; man has usurped the place and the rights of God, and to heal man's pride is the humility of God who for our sakes was made man. Little children assume that the world was made for them or, at least, that their little world should circle around them; their demands are imperious; their vexation, when they are thwarted, is a loud protest against the universe. They are not to be blamed. But many grown-up persons are still infants in this regard. They are indignant with life if it does not bring them what they want, they judge all men and things by reference to themselves and their advantage, they think it is God's *métier* to provide them with the satisfaction of heaven hereafter as well as with deliverance from troubles here. This is of the very essence of sin, because a man puts himself at the centre of the world, and the world's true centre is not man but God. Sin is pride, and virtue, therefore, is humility.

Not only do we tend to think of ourselves as the centre of the universe, but we have great pride in our attainments; we hold our heads up; we boast our respectability and claim to be respected by God as well as man. The prayer of the Pharisee (if it may be called a prayer), "Lord, I thank thee that I am not as other men are," is frequently in our hearts, if not on our lips, especially in these days of warfare against perversity and barbarism. But our pride must be broken before we can enter the low gate of heaven, and our redemption from sin is in no small part the breaking of our pride. To this end Christ took our flesh upon him and laboured in the carpenter's shop and was called the friend of publicans and sinners, "that all mankind should follow the example of his great humility." Human ambition soars upward, divine ambition is a condescension. There are some brave fellows, says St. Augustine, "who take credit to themselves not in respect of wealth or bodily strength nor any especial temporal powers of rank but in respect of their own goodness. This sort of brave people is to be avoided and feared and shunned, not imitated; for these people, I repeat, take credit to themselves not in respect of the body or possessions or family or office, for any one can see that things of this kind are temporary, transient, uncertain, volatile; no, they take credit for their goodness. It was this bravery that prevented the Jews from entering through the eye of a needle. For, when they were pluming themselves on being good and seemed to themselves to be, as it were, in fine health, they refused medicine and slew the Physician himself. Such brave folk, then, being in fine health, he did not come to call who said, 'They that are whole have no need of a physician but they that are sick; I came not to call the righteous but sinners to repentance.' These were the brave folk who taunted the disciples of Christ because their Master visited the sick and supped with them. 'Why,' said they, 'does your Master eat with publicans and sinners?' How brave are they who have no need of a physician! But that is the bravery not of health but of insanity! Nothing can be braver than a lunatic; he is far more powerful than the healthy; but the greater his strength, the nearer his death! God forbid that we imitate brave people of that sort!"

It is the Cross, and the Cross alone, that breaks our pride and thus slaying sin in us works our redemption. This is the distinction between the Gospel and philosophy. The pagans or neo-Platonists, says St. Augustine, had seen that all things are made by the Word of God, and even that God has an only-begotten Son through whom all things were made; "that truth they could see, but they saw it from afar; they refused the humility of Christ wherein as in a ship they could reach that which they were able to see afar; the Cross of Christ was mean to them. Here is a sea to be crossed, and thou spurnest the wooden transom? O proud wisdom, thou mockest Christ crucified; he it is whom thou sawest afar off. 'In the beginning was the Word, and the Word was with God.' But why was he crucified? Because the transom of his humility was necessary to thee. Thou wast swollen with pride, and far hadst thou been cast from that fatherland, and the way thereto was cut off by the waves of this world, and there was no means whereby passage might be made to the fatherland unless thou be carried by the transom. Ingrate, thou mockest him who cometh to thee that thou mayest return. He himself was made the way, and that, too, over the sea. For this he walked upon the sea, that he might shew there is a way upon the sea. But thou who by no means canst thyself walk upon the sea, be carried by the ship, be carried by the transom; believe in the crucified, and thou shalt be able to arrive. For thy sake was he crucified that he might teach humility."

The Cross of Christ has sometimes been preached as if he suffered that we might be delivered from all suffering. That is a shallow doctrine. "I am crucified with Christ," said the Apostle Paul. We are redeemed as we are made one with Christ in his redemptive activity. There is no way to heaven, says St. Thomas à Kempis, except "this royal road which is the road of the holy Cross." Why, then, he asks, dost thou fear to bear thy cross?, for that is the way into the kingdom. "In the cross is salvation, in the cross is life, in the cross is protection from the enemy; in the cross is infusion of supernal sweetness; in the cross is strength of purpose, in the cross is joy of spirit; in the cross is consummation of virtue, in the cross is perfection of sanctity. There is neither salvation of soul nor hope of life eternal save in the cross. Take up, therefore, thy cross and follow Jesus, and thou shalt go into life eternal. He went before carrying his cross, and died for thee upon the cross, that thou too shouldest bear thy cross and aspire to death upon the cross. For if thou shalt have died with him, with him too shalt thou likewise live; and if thou shalt have been his companion in his suffering, so shalt thou be also in his glory. . . . If thou bearest thy cross gladly, it shall bear thee, and shall bring thee to thy desired haven, where in truth shall be the end of suffering, though here it cannot be."

Here, as in St. Augustine, we have the image of the cross as that which must carry us to our goal. But what cross? Is it the historic cross of Calvary or the cross of individual suffering? At first sight the two crosses, the one historic, the other metaphorical, are confused, but we are here back in the same spiritual apprehension that we saw in St. John of Damascus. There is no real confusion, for the cross that is borne for Christ's sake is part of the suffering of Calvary for the redemption of the world. We are back, too, at that profound simplicity that our redemption is the return to God, and that Jesus Christ has come into the world to be the Way that, united with him, we might return to God.

CHAPTER VIII

The Middle Ages

Peter Abélard, who is first quoted, lived from A.D. 1079–1142. Treated as a heretic in his day he profoundly influenced all later medieval speculation. He interpreted the work of Christ as the awakening of love in us. St. Anselm, sometime Archbishop of Canterbury, lived from A.D. 1033–1109. He represented sin as being primarily an unpayable debt; the infinite merit of our Lord's sacrifice avails for its redemption. St. Thomas Aquinas, A.D. 1226–1274, was the greatest systematic theologian of the Middle Ages. He is here quoted as indicating the close connection between our Redemption and our membership in the Christian Church. Duns Scotus, the greatest and subtlest of Oxford theologians, lived from A.D. 1266–1308; he represents the Franciscan theology as St. Thomas the Dominican. Duns is here cited as laying stress upon the secret workings of God in our sanctification and redemption through the sacraments and discipline of the Church.

The tragic life of Abélard has been told in Miss Helen Waddell's novel *Peter Abélard* (Constable). St. Anselm's *Meditations* are published in Methuen's Library of Devotion. Franciscan thought is beautifully expressed in St. Bonaventura's *Itinerarium Mentis in Deum*, translated under the title of *The Franciscan Vision* (Burns, Oates). G. K. Chesterton wrote a life of St. Thomas Aquinas.

Questions that arise are such as these: (1) Is it sufficient to say that we are saved by Christ because he awakens in us the love of God? (2) Was the Incarnation necessary for our salvation? (3) How is the Church to be understood as the mystical Body of Christ? (4) How far does our salvation depend upon our conscious experience? (5) If the merit of Christ is infinite, shall it avail for all the sins of the whole world?

I

IT seems to us, however, that we are justified by the blood of Christ and reconciled to God in the following way: his Son took our nature and persevered in instructing us both in word and deed even unto death. This was the singular grace shown us, through which he more abundantly bound us to himself by love; so that set on fire as we are by so great a benefit from the Divine grace true charity should fear nothing at all. . . . And so our redemption is that supreme love manifested in our case by the passion of Christ, which not only delivers us from the bondage of sin, but also acquires for us the liberty of the sons of God; so that we may fulfil all things from the love rather than the fear of him, who, as he himself bears witness, showed us grace so great that no greater can be found. No man, says he, has greater love than this, that he lay down his life for his friends.

Such is the teaching of Peter Abélard in Dr. Franks' translation.

So St. Augustine might have written, but Abélard's doctrine, though sponsored in recent years by justly honoured names, is usually vilified by all those theologians who would be called orthodox. "No doubt," say they, "the story of Christ does in fact quicken in men's hearts the love of God, but that is all in the sphere of subjective feeling; so far as that is concerned, it would not matter whether in fact the story of Christ be true or false; only its result matters; this in effect is to cut the nerve of the Gospel." Karl Marx is reported to have said, "I am not myself a Marxist," and I hazard the opinion that Abélard himself did not hold the doctrine which is popularly called "Abelardian." But, if there be much left unsaid in the formulation cited above, it is true so far as it goes, and its spiritual insight is the more apparent when it is contrasted with the legalistic theory of the great Archbishop of Canterbury, St. Anselm, his contemporary. Abélard speaks directly to us to-day, while there is probably no traditional doctrine of Western Christendom less attractive to us now than that of St. Anselm.

II

Yet St. Anselm, for all his impersonal and legalistic language, saw deeper into the mystery of sin than Abélard. If it is largely St. Anselm who impressed upon our minds in the West the picture of an offended God requiring nothing less than the death of Christ before he would deliver man, we must not fail to overhear above the prosaic theology the overtones of a heart that is broken with the wonder and the grace of God. Thus in his *Meditation on the Redemption of Mankind*, as translated by Dr. C. C. J. Webb, he breaks out

Therefore, thou poor silly man, . . . consider what thou owest to thy Saviour. Remember how it was with thee, and what was done for thee, and consider how worthy is he of thy love, who did this for thee. Behold thy need and his goodness, and see what thanks thou shouldest render him, and how much thou owest unto his love. Thou wast in darkness, in a slippery place, in the way that goeth down into the pit of hell, whence is no returning; a huge weight as of lead hanging upon thy neck did drag thee downwards, thy back was bowed down by a burden thou wast not able to bear, invisible foes drove thee onward with all their might. . . . O good Lord Jesus, when I was thus set in the midst of these dangers and knew it not nor sought for deliverance, thou didst shine forth upon me like the sun, and show me in what state I stood. Thou didst cast away that leaden weight which dragged me downwards; thou didst remove the heavy burden which bowed me to the earth; thou didst drive away them that urged me forward and didst set thy face against them in my behalf. Thou didst call me by a new name which thou gavest me after thine own name. I was bowed together, and thou didst lift me up to look upon thy face, saying, Trust in me, I have redeemed thee, I have given my life for thee; if thou cleave to me thou shalt escape the evils which were about thee, and shalt not fall into the pit whither thou wast hastening; I will lead thee unto my Kingdom, and make thee an heir of God and joint heir with me.

This is the ecstatic language of St. Paul and St. Augustine and Luther and Bunyan. If St. Anselm's theology of redemption seems to us arid and legalistic, his heart was warm, and his sense of sin and of redemption was deep and experimental.

St. Anselm's most famous writing on our redemption, the *Cur Deus Homo*, is by no means homogeneous. That is, it has reminders and hints and suggestions that point to many different ways of regarding the subject, but his main argument may be summed up in this way: the Author of our redemption is God who shows his love for us in delivering us from sin, wrath hell, the power of the devil and bringing back for us the Kingdom of Heaven. The whole will of a rational creature ought to be subject to the will of God; that is the debt we owe God; our sin is our failure to pay that debt. But now we owe God more, for we owe something extra to make up for the insult we have offered to his majesty. What is the use of our penitence and contrition and fasting and labours, and acts of mercy and obedience now? For we owe this already. Even if we did not already owe it, it would not atone for sin, for about sin there is something infinite. The debt being infinite, only God can pay it; yet it must be paid by man; therefore it must be paid by one who is both God and man; hence the necessity for the Incarnation.

Such a summary does scant justice to a high and sustained argument, but it is certain that this theory will not satisfy us to-day. In the first place, sin may, indeed, be called a debt—"forgive us our debts, as we forgive our debtors"—but it is more than a debt; it is an inward perversion of the personality. In the second place, we, who have been taught about God in the parable of the Prodigal Son, can never be satisfied with a theory which seems to present God to us as the great Seigneur who is standing upon his rights. The earlier quotation from St. Anselm's *Meditations* shows how far he was from really thinking of man's relation to God in terms of private or public law; but reconciliation is so much more intimate and personal than the payment of a debt that any theological doctrine based upon the conception of the debtor-creditor relation falls far short of our needs.

St. Anselm adopts the curious view that the number of the elect from mankind is to make up the number of the fallen angels. The salvation offered by Christ, therefore, is available only for a limited number of mankind. But apart from this speculation there are hints which, had they been developed by St. Anselm, would have pointed in a contrary direction. The work of Christ, he tells us elsewhere, is concerned with the restoration of humanity; human nature is exalted in the Incarnation of our Lord; man's debt, indeed, is infinite, but our Lord's acceptance of death on our behalf outweighs all the sins of men; it is just, therefore, that God receiving that which is greater than the debt should wholly remit the debt. These hints, taken from different parts of the book, suggest to us, as indeed the doctrine of "original sin" implies, that all humanity is involved in the nexus of sin, and that all humanity is affected by the

Incarnation of our Lord. Furthermore, our Lord's death is of more weight than all the sins of all mankind; why, then, should not God in his mercy accept the sacrifice of Christ as payment for the whole debt of all and thus bring all men to his glory? But, if St. Anselm's heart sometimes indicated this answer, he could not so break with the traditional thought of his time, and the chief value of his treatise for us lies in his attempt to show on rational grounds the necessity of the Incarnation and in his deep sense of the burden of man's sin. If his theory is impersonal and legalistic, at least it is not shallow!

II

The followers of Karl Marx are wont to maintain that the cultural and political and intellectual movements of an age are simply a reflection of the economic order. They press this principle to absurdity, but the Middle Ages offers a good illustration of the fact that theology is often expressed in terms borrowed from the current social and political spheres. In those centuries men seemed naturally to express the work of Christ in terms of debt and merit; he paid our debt for us, he merited our salvation. The feudal system of the State on the one hand and the penitential system of the Church on the other provided the categories in which men spoke of their redemption. We cannot easily think in those terms. In particular, we would relate every doctrine to the Fatherhood and love of God and to our personal and filial relation to him. Here at least we seem to note theological advance. But religious advance is an altogether different matter. "She is forgiven much because she loved much" is a text that may be applied in the sphere of theology. We criticize as impersonal and unworthy the theological exposition of the grounds upon which the theologians of the Middle Ages based their love and gratitude; but do we with our more adequate categories and improved theological terms see as deeply as they did into the grace of God in Christ? The religion of the saints in every age shines through their theology, but because of the clear inadequacy of these categories of "debt" and "merit" we do not derive very great help in our thought from the medieval theologians.

St. Thomas Aquinas gathers up into his vast system all the hints and suggestions of previous ages; we cannot say of him that he offers any one single account of our redemption. In the main he expresses our faith in terms of Christ's meriting salvation for us by his voluntary death on our behalf, but it will suffice for our present purpose to indicate one aspect of our redemption which St. Thomas stresses more clearly than some of his predecessors, namely, the connection between our redemption and the Church.

He recognizes very fully that sin is much more than a debt. Sin, he says, consists in a disorder of the will; it is a radical malady of the personality. It consists in a man's cleaving to transient goods in contempt of God, whereas the merit of a good act consists in a man's cleaving to God as his end in contempt of created goods; that is, a man's true end is to glorify God and to do all things for the love of God; sin is action with a wrong or imperfect motive. The cause of sin is an inordinate love of oneself; it is self-centredness as opposed to God-centredness in the heart of man. Further, all humanity is a kind of corporate personality "in Adam"; that is how Adam's sin involves all mankind in sin. The Passion of Christ sets free the human race; his charity and obedience exceed the total offence of the human race. Why, then, may we not speak of a universal salvation merited and achieved by Christ? The answer must be that sin is a perversion of the personality; Christ's death is, indeed, says St. Thomas, a universal cause of salvation, but it must be applied in each individual case, and men may refuse its benefits if they refuse to cleave to God by faith and love. We are saved, therefore, as we respond to the grace of God in Christ and are ourselves united with the Passion of Christ by faith and charity and the sacraments. Sin is personal, therefore redemption must be personal, and it is to be worked out in the fellowship and under the discipline of the Christian Church.

But the Church is always to be conceived as the Body of Christ; in the Church we are united to him by faith and charity and by receiving his divine life into ourselves. Thus the Passion of Christ moves us to charity, as Abélard taught, and, beyond

Abélard, "the whole Church which is the mystical Body of Christ, is reckoned as one person with Christ as its head."

We are far from understanding, still farther from a complete and tidy theory, but here various aspects of our redemption stand out clearly. First, God is the author of our redemption; second, our sin and alienation from God is something from which we could not deliver ourselves; Christ has delivered us by taking our nature and accepting the Cross for us; third, since sin is a perversion of our personality, it can only be overcome as we ourselves are changed; we must come to love God where now we love ourselves; this change takes place in us as in the Church we are incorporated into Christ; our redemption is at once sure, since we belong to Christ, and incomplete while we are still imperfect.

So far so good, but the Middle Ages is the period of Christendom when the nations of Europe were included in the Church, and the far lands of the heathen were little in men's thoughts except as the dwellings of the infidels, who were somehow regarded as responsible for their infidelity. It was possible to think, or at least to hope, that all men being baptized into the Church and being more or less subject to the Church would, unless by apostasy they denied their Saviour, attain by his merits in the end to everlasting life. We live in a secular age. If we may rightly still regard our country as a Christian land because Christian principles and a Christian outlook are still widely accepted, we must recognize that of our fellows only a minority are in any effective contact with the Church. Moreover, the shrinkage of the world through new means of transport and communication has raised for us in an acute form the relation of the work of Christ to all humanity. Are we to think that his death has been in vain in respect of the vast majority of mankind? We cannot think of the world outside the Church as consisting solely of wilful and deliberate unbelievers, nor do we think of Christians as necessarily being morally superior to those who make no profession of Christ's name. We are bound to the world outside not merely by knowledge, but also by affection. If our love goes out to these, how much more the love of God! Under the stress of such considerations as these many have virtually ceased to believe in our redemption through Christ's Incarnation, Death and Resurrection, since they cannot with any reality say either that Christ's work affects those who make no response to it, or that the love of God is thwarted because in this life men have not responded to it.

III

Our modern problem did not wholly escape the notice of the subtlest of all the theologians, the great Oxford scholar, Duns Scotus, but his answer to it certainly does not help us greatly. Christ, he says, is the Head of all men—but in different ways, "for, although he redeemed all men by his Passion, and thus is made the Saviour of all (for, as he finds none free from liability to punishment, so he comes for the salvation of all), yet he did not merit salvation for all in the same way, nor did he offer his Passion to the Trinity with like efficacy in all cases, nor was it accepted in all cases in the same way; otherwise all would be saved, whereas it is agreed that most are damned." In the case of those who were not elect Christ offered his Passion in such a way that it would have sufficed to achieve their salvation, but, because they were to be damned as a result of their malice, his Passion was not offered efficaciously nor, in consequence, was it accepted; thus he is Head of the elect and of the reprobate in different ways.

Unsatisfactory as this is, it points to the two principles which the period grasped securely, namely, that God's justice must be vindicated, and that redemption must be related to actual progress in grace. Duns uses many terms in which to speak of the redeeming work of Christ—satisfaction of the divine justice, merit, sacrifice, redemption; here he has nothing strikingly new to say, but he is of especial interest to us as laying more than most a stress upon the sacraments of the Church in the work of our redemption, or, we might better say, upon the sacramental system, for he has primarily in mind the sacraments of baptism and penance. When Duns speaks of the sacraments he tends to have in mind both what we have to do and what God does mysteriously in our hearts. There is no doubt a danger lest we fall into the heresy of supposing that we can be saved by our own moral efforts, a heresy to which the British seem peculiarly prone, but it is part of the strength of our Western tradition that it insists that we ourselves must overcome the devil within ourselves if we are to be redeemed.

But Duns was far indeed from preaching "justification by works." We are delivered from the power of the devil, he says, by the passion and death of Christ. Then he adds, we are delivered from the power of the devil by the sacrament of penance which was instituted by Christ and derives its efficacy from his Passion. That is to say, the sacraments and ordinances of the Church are the appointed means by which God works his saving work within us, by them we are led by the hand to things invisible; Christ's Passion takes away the cause of sins, but not the effect; sacraments, therefore, are given us to be efficacious signs of grace; they are, as he elsewhere calls them, practical signs; they do not act physically like a drug in the body, but by God's grace they infallibly produce their effect if they be duly used and received. Through the life and ordinances of the Church God imprints a "character" or spiritual quality on the soul. This language may seem strange to us, but Duns is stressing a matter of great importance. The work of grace goes on in our hearts secretly if we do not resist it; in the life of the Church we grow, and we may be as unconscious of our spiritual growth as of our physical. The redemption wrought by Christ is not magic, neither are the sacraments and ordinances magic, but they represent, and are the appointed channels of, that mysterious and blessed work of the Holy Spirit in our redemption which goes on in the secret places of our hearts and below the level of our consciousness.

The sacraments are efficacious not in themselves as rites, but because it has pleased God to ordain them as means of grace. But God is not confined in his action to the Christian sacraments. The sacraments of the Old Testament also, says Duns, were efficacious signs of grace, and in the rite of circumcision God granted sanctifying grace for the blotting out of original sin. Baptism is the appointed means of grace. It is God's means, not his limitation, as small minds so often have supposed. "No one can be saved without baptism either in fact and effect, or in desire and affect," says Duns; thus, where there is desire but no minister, or in the case of those who have no knowledge of the sacraments but conform their actions to the law of nature written in their hearts and live according to reason the unbaptized are as if they had been baptized. We cannot make too much of the sacraments as means of grace, but we fall into sin if we claim that the grace of God in our redemption must be confined to them.

In this chapter on the Middle Ages four points for meditation have been raised or raised again. First, we are redeemed as by the grace of God in Christ the love of God is kindled in our hearts and we are won from the world to God; second, we have considered again how grievous a burden, how inescapable a bondage, how unpayable a debt is sin, and how lost and helpless we are apart from the amazing grace of God in the Cross and Passion of our Lord; third, we are redeemed as members of the Church, that is, of the Body of Christ; the Church is not merely the sphere of grace, it is also the life of Christ in the souls of men; we are redeemed because Christ has identified himself with us, and we have responded with faith and love; fourth, it has pleased God in his infinite wisdom and mercy to ordain the sacraments and ordinances of the Church as signs and channels of his grace, not that they may limit him, but that they may save us.

CHAPTER IX

The Reformation

The Reformation represents a fresh apprehension of the grace of God in the forgiveness of our sins. It is Augustinian in that it stresses the divine initiative of grace and declares the impotence of man in any way to commend himself to God. Forgiveness is made the beginning of the Christian life, and the two Pauline terms "grace" and "peace" are made to cover the essentials of the Gospel message. Redemption is a personal relationship between the gracious God and the forgiven sinner. This is illustrated from Luther, Bunyan, Hooker and others.

Books that may be consulted are (1) *Reformation Writings*, by Martin Luther (Lutterworth Press); (2) *Grace Abounding to the Chief of Sinners*, by John Bunyan; (3) Richard Hooker, *Sermon II*; (4) John Wesley's *Journal*.

Questions for discussion: (1) What place, if any, is there for the notion of human merit before God? (2) What does Luther mean by calling faith "the wedding ring"? (3) What is the relation between "justification by faith" and good works? (4) Is the doctrine of "imputed righteousness" a legalistic or a strictly religious notion, and how is it to be understood? (5) Did the Reformation bring anything new in the way of doctrine or experience?

THE Protestant Reformation can be viewed from many angles, as a great simplification of theology, as an ethical reform of corruptions in the Church, as a schism within the Church, as the spiritual uprising of the northern nations, as the religious expression of the new nationalism. Or, again, the Reformation may be viewed in its supposed consequences, the rise of the Capitalist order, the disruption of medieval Christendom, the moralism and intellectual aridity into which at certain periods it fell; indeed, Protestantism is sometimes represented as responsible for the chaos of the modern world, for the war and even for Adolf Hitler.

I

This is no place for a defence of Protestantism, but even its enemies must realize that it represents (though too often it fails to embody) a profound religious apprehension. It has been said of Luther that he was a heretic in this unique sense that he grasped one aspect of the catholic faith with such tenacity and saw it in so bright a light that he was blinded to every other aspect of the truth. This one truth which Luther grasped was directly connected with the doctrine of redemption.

The Fathers of the medieval Western Church had laid great stress upon the necessity of penance as a supplement to the work of Christ in our redemption. Faith in the saving work of Christ and the power of the sacraments must be supplemented by self-discipline and good works. The epistles of St. Paul must not be interpreted apart from the epistle of St. James. To some extent, therefore, it was taught that man must not only "work out" his own salvation, but even, in part at least, achieve it. Moreover, the Church in the sixteenth century was appallingly corrupt. A particularly scandalous illustration of this was the hawking of certificates the purchase of which, it was alleged, would relieve the owner of so much suffering in purgatory hereafter. These so-called Indulgences; which were an important source of revenue to the Papacy, were an offence to any spiritually-minded person. These Indulgences coupled with the insistence upon works as necessary to salvation and with an often superstitious trust in the irresistible efficacy of sacraments obscured the Gospel promises of the divine forgiveness and of the nature of redemption as a personal reconciliation of the sinner with his God.

The Indulgences were an offence to decency, but, deeper than that, Luther had discovered in his own tortured experience how impossible it is for man, try as he will, to establish his own righteousness before God. A monastic form of absolution common in his time, as he tells us, was this: "God forgive thee, my brother. The merit of the passion of our Lord Jesus Christ, and of blessed St. Mary, always a Virgin, and of all the saints: the merit of thine order, the straitness of thy religion, the humility of thy confession, the contrition of thy heart, the good works which thou hast done and shalt do for the love of our Lord Jesus Christ, be unto thee available for the remission of thy sins, the increase of desert and grace, and the reward of everlasting life. Amen."

It would be unfair to take this formula as a careful theological statement, but the language accurately expresses the Church outlook of the time. The redeeming work of Christ is not denied, but his Passion is expressed in impersonal terms of merit rather than in terms of evoking love, and salvation is plainly deemed to depend at least in part upon man himself and his own efforts. But what of a man who in spite of all his efforts could not satisfy himself, much less God? Of the rules and regulations laid down by the Church Luther says, "I endeavoured to observe and keep them myself as much as was possible for me to do; punishing my poor body with fasting, watching, praying and other exercises, more than all they who at this day do so bitterly hate and persecute me." The devil, he said, was his best schoolmaster in divinity, for it was the devil who taught him the sinfulness and impotence of man and thus cast him back upon the grace of Christ alone. The grace of Christ brings peace to the troubled heart:

> these two words, grace and peace [he writes (ad Gal. i. 3)] do contain in them the whole sum of Christianity. Grace containeth the remission of sins, peace, a quiet and joyful conscience. But peace of conscience can never be had, unless sin be first forgiven. But sin is not forgiven for the fulfilling of the law; for no man is able to satisfy the law. But the law doth rather show sin, accuse and terrify the conscience, declare the wrath of God, and drive to desperation. Much less is sin taken away by the works and inventions of men. . . . But when the grace and peace of God are in the heart, then is man strong, so that he can neither be cast down with adversity, nor puffed up with prosperity, but walketh on plainly, and keepeth the highway. For he taketh heart and courage in the victory of Christ's death; and the confidence thereof beginneth to reign in his conscience over sin and death, because through him he hath assured forgiveness of his sins; which, after he hath once obtained, his conscience is at rest, and by the word of grace is comforted.

Protestantism is a revival of Augustinianism on its evangelical side. Luther's experience was like that of St. Augustine; for both the grace of Christ to sinners is the heart of the Gospel.

We can only understand Luther as in some degree we have ourselves known the despair of making ourselves good and thus commending ourselves to God. We must be forgiven and reconciled to God as the beginning of the life in Christ. The form of absolution cited above implies that, if we can commend ourselves to God by our conduct, then in virtue of Christ's death, we may hope for heaven hereafter. Luther said, on the contrary, if we trust in Christ, we know ourselves forgiven now, and our salvation depends upon Christ alone, not in any degree upon our commending ourselves to God. Of course, Luther does not mean that our conduct and moral effort do not matter; but the Christian life springs out of our forgiveness; it is not the condition of our forgiveness.

Commenting on the words, "which gave himself for our sins," Luther says:

Weigh diligently every word of Paul, and specially mark well this pronoun, *our*; for the effect altogether consisteth in the well applying of the pronouns, which we find very often in the Scriptures; wherein also there is ever some vehemency and power. . . . Without the pronoun it is an easy matter to magnify and amplify the benefit of Christ, namely, that Christ was given for sins, but for other men's sins, which are worthy. But when it cometh to the putting to of this pronoun *our*, there our weak nature and reason starteth back, and dare not come nigh unto God, nor promise to herself, that so great a treasure shall be freely given unto her, and therefore she will not have to do with God except first she be pure and without sin; wherefore, although she read or hear this sentence, "who gave himself for our sins" or such like, yet doth she not apply this pronoun (our) unto herself, but unto others which are worthy and holy; and as for herself, she will tarry till she be made worthy by her own works. . . . I say this not for nought, for I have oftentimes proved by experience, and I daily find, what a hard matter it is to believe (especially in the conflict of conscience) "that Christ was given," not for the holy, righteous, worthy, and such as were his friends, "but for wicked sinners, for the unworthy, and for his enemies, which have deserved God's wrath and everlasting death." Let us, therefore, arm ourselves with these and suchlike sentences of the Holy Scripture, that we may be able to answer the devil (accusing us and saying, "thou art a sinner, and therefore thou art damned"), in this sort: Because thou sayest I am a sinner, therefore will I be righteous and saved. Nay (saith the devil) "thou shalt be damned." No, (say I) for I fly unto Christ, "who hath given himself for my sins;" therefore, Satan, "thou shalt not prevail against me," in that thou goest about to terrify me, in setting forth the greatness of my sins, and so to bring me into heaviness, distrust, despair, hatred, contempt, and blaspheming of God. Yea rather, in that thou sayest, I am a sinner, thou givest me armour and weapon against thyself, that with thine own sword I may cut thy throat, and tread thee under my feet; for Christ died for sinners. Moreover, thou thyself preachest unto me the glory of God; for thou puttest me in mind of God's fatherly love towards me, wretched and damned sinner, "Who so loved the world that he gave his only-begotten Son, that whosoever believeth in him shall not perish, but have everlasting life." And, as often as thou objectest that I am a sinner, so often thou callest me to remembrance of the benefit of Christ my Redeemer, upon whose shoulders, and not upon mine, lie all my sins; for the Lord hath "laid all our iniquity upon him." Again, "for the transgressions of his people was he smitten." Wherefore, when thou sayest I am a sinner, thou dost not terrify me, but comfort me above measure.

It was by no accident that John Wesley was converted by hearing the words of Luther. He writes in his *Journal* under the date May 24, 1738:

In the evening I went very unwillingly to a society in Aldersgate Street, where one was reading Luther's preface to the Epistle to the Romans. About a quarter before nine, while he was describing the change which God works in the heart through faith in Christ, I felt my heart strangely warmed. I felt I did trust in Christ, Christ alone, for salvation; and an assurance was given me that he had taken away my sins, even mine, and saved me from the law of sin and death."

The theological dispute at the Reformation centred upon the term "justification"; the Romanists took it in its Latin sense to mean "making just"; the Protestants, here actually nearer to the meaning of St. Paul, understood by justification both acceptance and forgiveness. That which the Romanists called justification they called sanctification. It may appear to us, as it appeared to many in those days, that the two sides were contending for contradictory truths. The Protestants were not enunciating a novel doctrine, but one that had been overlaid. Their experience, often called "the evangelical experience," was not something unknown in the Middle Ages, but it became the typical experience of Protestantism and determinative of its theology.

Of this "evangelical experience" one classical illustration may be quoted. John Bunyan wrote in his autobiography, *Grace Abounding to the Chief of Sinners*:

> Now I was sick in my inward man, my soul was clogged with guilt; now also was my former experience of God's goodness to me quite taken out of my mind, and hid as if they had never been or seen; now was my soul greatly pitched between these two considerations, *Live I must not! Die I dare not;* now I sunk and fell in my spirit and was giving up all for lost; but, as I was walking up and down in the house, as a man in a most woeful state, that Word of God took hold of my heart, *Ye are justified freely by his grace through the redemption that is in Christ Jesus.* But oh! what a turn it made upon me! Now was I awakened as one out of some troublesome sleep and dream; and listening to this heavenly sentence, I was as if I had heard it thus spoken to me: "Sinner, thou thinkest that because of thy sins and infirmities I cannot save thy soul; but, behold, my Son is by me, and upon him I look, and not on thee, and shall deal with thee according as I am pleased with him." At this I was greatly enlightened in my mind and made to understand that God could justify a sinner at any time; it was but his looking upon Christ and imputing of his benefits to us, and the Word was forthwith done.

We may recall a close parallel to that last sentence from a saint of a very different tradition. This is how Canon Bright puts it in his great Communion hymn:

> Look, Father, look on his anointed face,
> And only look on us as found in him;
> Look not on our misusings of thy grace,
> Our prayer so languid, and our faith so dim:
> For lo! between our sins and their reward
> We set the Passion of thy Son our Lord.

The "evangelical experience" is not the perquisite only of those who stand in the so-called Evangelical tradition; it is catholic, in the sense, not that it is the universal experience of all Christians, but that it is common to unnumbered Christians from different ages and different theological persuasions. Bunyan puts the matter in the simple language of the countryside, but the same overwhelming experience underlies the more theological but not less passionate words of Richard Hooker, never more judicious than when he wrote:

> Christ hath merited righteousness for as many as shall be found in him. And in him God findeth us, if we are true believers, for by faith we are incorporated into Christ. Then, although we be altogether sinful and unrighteous in ourselves, yet even the man who is in himself ungodly, full of iniquity, full of sin, him being found in Christ through faith and having his sin in hatred through repentance, him God beholdeth with a gracious eye, putteth away his sin by not imputing it, taketh quite away the punishment due thereto by pardoning it, and accepteth him in Christ Jesus as if he had fulfilled all that is commanded in the law, shall I say more perfectly righteous than if himself had fulfilled all the law? I must take heed what I say, but the Apostle saith, God made him to be sin for us, who knew no sin, that we might be made the righteousness of God in him. Such we are, then, in the sight of God as is the very Son of God himself. Let it be counted folly or phrensy or fury or whatever; it is our wisdom and our comfort. We care for no knowledge in the whole world but this: that man hath sinned, and God hath suffered, that God hath made himself the sin of men, and that men are made the righteousness of God.

II

We may say that the Reformation brought no new doctrine, but it marked a vivid and life-giving rediscovery of aspects of the Christian life and faith which had been set out of perspective or overlaid. Three elements in particular in this new presentation of our redemption deserve comment and consideration.

First, our redemption is conceived in terms of mere acceptance by the exercise of faith. The Passion of Christ may still be interpreted in terms of merit, but all thought of human merit is indignantly repudiated. "I must say I never have had so close and satisfactory a view of the Gospel salvation," said Thomas Chalmers, the great Scottish divine, "as when I have been led to contemplate it in the light of a simple offer on the one side, and a simple acceptance on the other." God, in the Apostle's phrase, is he "that justifieth the ungodly." This does not mean that God pretends the sinner is just when he is not, nor does it mean, in the first instance, that God makes the unjust to become just; rather it means that for Christ's sake God receives the sinner just as he is, freely forgives him, and brings him home to himself. All that is required of the sinner is that he accept the good news: for "while he was yet afar off, his father saw him, and was moved with compassion, and ran, and fell on his neck, and kissed him . . . for this my son was dead and is alive again; he was lost, and is found." Forgiveness upon the basis of Christ's death for us is not merely the end of the story if we persevere and commend ourselves by our good conduct; it is the beginning of the story also; we are forgiven now, just as we are, if with faith and love and penitence we turn to a forgiving and all-powerful Saviour.

It is sometimes said that this is an immoral doctrine, or, at least, that it neglects the moral demands and conditions apart from which there can be no real redemption. No doubt the doctrine of immediate and full forgiveness on the basis of faith alone has sometimes been carelessly and misleadingly stated; but the difference between the new doctrine and the old was not that in the new there was no place for the works of righteousness, but that these works were deemed the fruits of forgiveness and not the basis upon which forgiveness was to be expected. Good works, to be acceptable to God, must be the fruits of the Spirit which is given with forgiveness.

The practical lesson, the first learning of which is conversion, and which has to be relearned and better learned all the days of our life, wrote Professor A. G. Hogg, is to be willing to take this gift on God's terms, i.e. freely, without in any way or degree earning it. . . . If we are honest, we find it a spiritual impossibility to be willing to accept this costly forgiveness as a simple gift, until we consciously surrender all claim to reckon ourselves henceforward our own.

The same matter is put in more solemn language by Richard Hooker:

> We teach, he says, that faith alone justified, but we by this speech never meant to exclude either hope and charity from being alway joined as inseparable mates with faith in the man that is justified or works from being added as necessary duties, required at the hands of every justified man: but to show that faith is the only hand which putteth on Christ unto justification; and Christ the only garment which, being so put on, covereth the shame of our defiled natures, hideth the imperfections of our works, preserveth us blameless in the sight of God, before whom otherwise the very weakness of our faith were cause sufficient to make us culpable yea, to shut us out from the kingdom of heaven, where nothing that is not absolute can enter.

III

Second, it will be observed that, while "faith" here certainly has an intellectual content, being faith in the redeeming work of Christ on Calvary, yet the word connotes essentially personal trust in a personal Saviour, and is no mere acceptance of a creed or hope. Formal Protestant theology was still in relatively impersonal terms such as debt and merit and sacrifice, but at the heart of it was a new personal relationship to God through Christ. This Protestant use of the term "faith" to express personal trust in a Person has full New Testament warrant, but is one of the many sources of misunderstanding between Protestants and Romanists; for the latter normally mean by "faith" a virtue of the intellect whereby we believe the truths of our religion. This virtue by itself and without love, they say, is of small avail; in their theology, therefore, they speak much of the love of God. In the terminology of the Protestants, on the other hand, love is included in faith, which Luther once called "the wedding ring" uniting the soul to Christ. The fact that Romanists and Protestants use different terms does not necessarily mean that their apprehension of our Lord is different. But this realization of personal forgiveness and of justification by personal trust alone (apart from works) is typical of Protestantism because, rightly or wrongly, it was made the starting point of Church theology.

IV

Third, in the passages quoted above we come upon the perplexing notion of "the imputed righteousness" of Christ; that is, Christ's righteousness is said to be given to us, Christ, as Richard Hooker puts it following St. Paul, being made sin for us that we should be made the righteousness of God in him. This is a doctrine which is readily mis-stated and misunderstood. It is simply a new form of a spiritual apprehension which we have considered in earlier chapters. We may appear before God because we are "in Christ"; he is our Representative, the head of the new humanity which he has redeemed; he, moreover, is the true life of the Church; we are saved because Christ is both for us and in us. In older forms, while we may suppose the meaning was the same, the idea was expressed in somewhat impersonal terms, as if Christ saved us by taking to himself our human nature or by offering himself as sacrifice on our behalf or as working upon our nature through the sacraments. In the new form it might seem to be suggested that God pretends we are not what we are. There are, therefore, objections to all these expressions, but all declare the fact that we are saved because we are united to Christ, and thus Christ becomes our real life. This was classically expressed by a Scottish Episcopalian of the seventeenth century, Henry Scougal: "True religion is an union of the soul with God, a real participation of the divine nature, the very image of God drawn upon the soul; or, in the Apostle's phrase, it is Christ formed within us. Briefly, I know not how the nature of religion can be more fully expressed than by calling it a divine life."

In this chapter redemption has been considered rather as a present possession than as a future beatitude; and this corresponds with the passionate sense that already we are forgiven, already we are passed from death to life; the Kingdom of God is here. But this was not to the forgetting of the hope of everlasting life. The passage quoted above from John Bunyan continues:

And as I was thus in a muse, that Scripture also came with great power upon my spirit, *Not by works of righteousness that we have done, but according to his mercy he hath saved us*, etc. Now was I got on high, I saw myself within the arms of Grace and Mercy; and, though I was before afraid to think of a dying hour, yet now I cried, "Let me die;" now death was lovely and beautiful in my sight, for I saw, *we shall never live indeed, till we be gone to the other world*. Oh! methought this life is but a slumber, in comparison of that above. At this time also I saw more in these words, *heirs of God*, than ever I shall be able to express while I live in this world; *heirs of God!* God himself is the portion of the saints. This I saw and wondered at, but cannot tell you what I saw.

Yet the present experience of a joyful salvation and full assurance of faith are the distinctive characteristics of this type of piety. We must not suppose, however, that this happiness and joy are unclouded even for the greatest saints. I close the chapter with one final quotation from John Bunyan; he had been depressed and ill and could not feel his soul to move or stir after grace and life by Christ:

After I had been in this condition some three or four days, as I was sitting by the fire, I suddenly felt this word to sound in my heart, "I must go to Jesus": at this my former darkness and atheism fled away, and the blessed things of heaven were set in my view. While I was on this sudden thus overtaken with surprise, Wife, said I, is there ever such a Scripture, "I must go to Jesus"? She said, she could not tell; therefore I stood musing still, to see if I could remember such a place: I had not sat above two or three minutes, but that came bolting in on me, "and to an innumerable company of angels"; and withal the twelfth chapter of Hebrews, about the Mount Sion was set before mine eyes. Then with joy I told my wife, "O, now I know, I know!" But that night was a good night to me, I never had but few better; I longed for the company of some of God's people, that I might have imparted unto them what God had showed me. Christ was a precious Christ to my soul that night; I could scarce lie in bed for joy, and peace, and triumph, through Christ. This great glory did not continue upon me until morning, yet the twelfth chapter of the epistle to the Hebrews, Heb. xii. 22, 23, was a blessed Scripture to me for many days together after this.

WHAT is the upshot, then, of the whole matter? It is, I think, twofold. In the first place, if we believe that we are re-deemed by Christ, we must realise that we have only begun to enter into the understanding and experience of that redemption which even in this world is available to those who love God with all their heart and mind and soul and strength. In the second place, it will, I hope, have become plain that no single human theory is adequate to explain or even reveal the wonder of God's grace to us in our Lord Jesus Christ. We can only apprehend "with all saints" and with all theologies "the breadth and length and depth and height and know the love of Christ which passeth knowledge."

If I may be permitted a personal word, it must be this: I write these lines sitting in the shade of the garden under a blue sky and surrounded by the sounds and scents of an English summer. While I write here, there are raging unimaginable battles on the Libyan desert, on the Russian steppes, in China, on land and sea and in the air. Am I only concerned with my own soul? And, if I say of those dying upon the battlefields, "What, Lord of them?" does he only say to me, "What is that to thee? Follow thou me?" Does he not also say, "Them also must I bring?" The salvation of God must come home to the indi-vidual soul; that I know. Christ is the Head of the Church which is his Body, the company of the redeemed; I know that too. But, when I think of those now fighting and dying, I think that Christ is more than the Saviour of those who trust in him, more than the Saviour of the Church; he is the Saviour of the world; he effected a cosmic salvation. It is the eternal purpose of God in him to sum up all things both which are in heaven and which are in earth, even in him in whom we have redemp-tion through his blood. I cannot believe that those now dying there, mostly in ignorance of his saving Name, are passing beyond the scope and efficacy of his redeeming blood. Do not misunderstand me, as if I meant there is no "hell." I am sure

95

that "hell" is a terrible, unimaginable reality. But neither in our own case nor in the case of these strangers may we so belittle Christ as to question his power to save. For a thousand years the theologians have been chiefly concerned with the salvation of those who believe. I judge that our new sense of social solidarity and the agonies of the present hour are forcing us back to neglected elements in the teaching of the Bible and in the theology of those Fathers, especially in the East, who expounded for us what it means that our Lord took our human nature upon him and thus became the Saviour of the world.

Finally, our Redemption is the work of the whole Trinity. Forgetfulness of this has led to error and misjudgment. Thus, all theologians agree that our redemption springs from the eternal will of our heavenly Father, but many have declared that God might, had it pleased him, have saved us without the Cross of Christ and the ministries of the Church; these have failed to recognise in sin an inner perversion of the personality and in salvation a personal reconciliation with a personal God. Others, again, have so stressed the work of Christ on Calvary as, in effect, to deny the work of the Holy Ghost in our redemption; they have insufficiently reckoned that there can be no effective work of Christ *for* us that is not also a work *in* us; they have stressed the death of Christ to the relative neglect of the living Christ with whom we must be united. Others, finally, have seen in redemption little more than the sanctifying work of the Holy Ghost and have denied or overlooked the Incarnation and the dying Victory of Christ. The grace of God is too large for our finite minds. We can but dimly apprehend one aspect of it at a time; but to Father, Son and Holy Ghost, one God, blessed for ever we give thanks, and for ever shall give thanks, for our redemption.